summersdale

D1808290

THE
CONSPIRACY
THEORY
TRIVIA BOOK

A Deep Dive into the
World's Most Puzzling
Secrets with Trivia
Questions, Fascinating
Facts and More...

JAMIE KING

An Hachette UK Company
www.hachette.co.uk

Summersdale Publishers
Part of Octopus Publishing Group Limited
Carmelite House
50 Victoria Embankment
LONDON
EC4Y 0DZ
UK

This FSC® label means that materials used for the product have been responsibly sourced

MIX
Paper | Supporting responsible forestry
FSC® C016973

www.summersdale.com

The authorized representative in the EEA is Hachette Ireland, 8 Castlecourt Centre, Castleknock Road, Castleknock, Dublin 15, D15 YF6A, Ireland

Printed and bound in Malaysia

ISBN: 978-1-83799-515-8

Substantial discounts on bulk quantities of Summersdale books are available to corporations, professional associations and other organizations. For details contact general enquiries: telephone: +44 (0) 1243 771107 or email: enquiries@summersdale.com.

Important note: The conspiracy theories contained in this book are just that: theories. The editor and the publishers make no claim that any of these theories have any basis in fact. They are merely theories that have at some point been expressed in the public domain. Such theories are reproduced herein for entertainment purposes only and are not intended to be taken literally.

CONTENTS

INTRODUCTION

Welcome to *The Conspiracy Theory Trivia Book*, your guide to nearly a hundred incredible conspiracy theories, including tales of extraterrestrials, government secrets and ancient mysteries.

Have you ever looked at the night sky and wondered if we're truly alone? Or perhaps you've questioned the official narrative of a historical event. You need wonder no longer, as we reveal the fascinating (and sometimes eyebrow-raising) world of conspiracy theories.

Whether you're a seasoned conspiracy theorist or just want to find out more, this book is your guide to navigating the murky waters of hidden truths and secret plots. And to add to the fun, each chapter features a quiz for you to test your new-found knowledge. From Roswell aliens to the disappearance of Finland, we'll examine the theories and lay out the facts so that you can make up your own mind about what really happened.

CHAPTER ONE
THE
CLASSICS

Have you ever wondered whether that "giant leap for mankind" took place on the Moon or in a Hollywood studio? Or asked yourself what's really in the white trails left by airplanes in an otherwise clear blue sky?

In this chapter, we look at classic conspiracy theories, both big and small, including some juicy mysteries that have sparked debate for decades. From reports of Hitler's escape to a base on the dark side of the Moon, to chilling rumours of government mind control and presidential assassinations, we explore the iconic theories that continue to ignite curiosity and raise eyebrows across the world.

THE MOON LANDING

The Moon landing's authenticity has long been questioned by conspiracy theorists. Millions of people across the world watched Neil Armstrong take his first "giant leap" in 1969 – but was it on the Moon or in a Hollywood studio lot?

You do not have to look far to find motivation for faking the landing. In the late 60s, the space race between the US and the USSR was gripping the world, a deadly serious geopolitical rivalry.

However, scientists say that creating the footage in a cinema studio and keeping the project secret would have been an even greater challenge than reaching the Moon in a rocket, given the crude special effects in movies at that time.

THREE KEY QUESTIONS THAT CONSPIRACISTS ARE ASKING:

- Why does the flag flutter, given that there is no wind in space?
- Why are the shadows at strange angles, when there is only one light source in space, the Sun?
- Why do photographs taken on the Moon show very few stars when they should be everywhere?

FLUORIDE

Is the government secretly dosing us with mind-controlling chemicals disguised as cavity fighters? Is fluoride, which is meant to fortify our teeth, actually dissolving our bones?

Conspiracy theories have simmered around water fluoridation for decades, painting it as a silent weapon, perhaps for population control. Some believe it is a communist plot, while others blame the aluminium industry for using the water system to dispose of their waste fluoride. What conspiracists do agree on is that something sinister is lurking in this seemingly harmless mineral.

There's no doubt that fluoride hardens teeth, but it is fatal in high enough doses. Some conspiracy theorists believe that long-term ingestion of fluoride causes genetic damage, causing teeth and bones to dissolve. This damage is then passed on to the next generation, who suffer more damage from fluoride, and so on. Chillingly, conspiracists speculate that a child could be born without a skeleton within seven generations.

CHEMTRAILS

Look up on a clear day and you'll see white lines criss-crossing the sky, created by passing airplanes. According to scientists, these contrails are formed naturally by water vapour and ice crystals. However, some conspiracy theorists believe these lines are actually chemtrails, evidence of dangerous chemicals being sprayed over populations all over the world.

CHEMTRAIL THEORIES

- Population control: Could chemtrails be a sinister tool to curb overpopulation, sprayed by a hidden government organization to control our numbers, spreading new diseases such as SARS, H1N1 and Covid-19?

- Climate cover-up: Some believe profit-hungry corporations are using chemtrails to mask the true effects of global warming by dimming the planet with clouds of sulphur.

- Weather weapon: Others theorize that chemtrails are part of a US government weather-control programme, used to trigger disasters like the Boxing Day tsunami and Hurricane Katrina in order to boost oil prices.

HITLER'S MOON BASE

According to the history books, Adolf Hitler died by suicide in April 1945, in his underground bunker in Berlin. Soviet forces were closing in on Berlin, and Germany was on the brink of defeat. Witness statements and dental records confirmed his identity but there is an alternative theory: that this was a ruse to cover up the evil dictator's escape, along with his long-time mistress, Eva Braun.

Conspiracy theorists have long speculated that Hitler fled to Argentina or Antarctica to live out the remainder of his days in luxury, financed by Nazi gold plundered during World War Two. However, these are nothing compared to a third theory, which is that he escaped on a rocket to a secret colony on the dark side of the Moon.

Supporters of the Moon-base theory say that this is backed up by a number of key facts. Nazi scientists had already developed the V-2 rocket, the first long-range guided ballistic missile. They were undoubtedly working on even more advanced projects before the end of the war, and many of them were later heavily involved in the US and Soviet space programmes.

THE EVERLASTING LIGHT BULB

Consider the humble light bulb. There are no moving parts: electricity goes in and light comes out. So why did the original light bulbs last such a short time? And why, even with today's technological advances, do we still need to replace them every few years?

According to one theory, the answer is straightforward: profit. Conspiracy theorists claim that a secret cartel of light-bulb manufacturers, formed in 1924, deliberately shortened the lifespan of light bulbs to increase profits. The Phoebus cartel, as it was called, agreed to weaken the filaments, the crucial component in a light bulb, to ensure more frequent replacements.

Conspiracists point to the so-called "Centennial Light", a light bulb that has been shining since 1901 at the Livermore-Pleasanton Fire Department in California. As longer lifespans were possible over a hundred years ago, the question remains: why are we still replacing our light bulbs today?

THE CENTENNIAL LIGHT

The Centennial Light is a hand-blown, carbon-filament light bulb that has been burning continuously since 1901. It holds the Guinness World Record for the world's longest-lasting incandescent light bulb.

MK-ULTRA

MK-Ultra was a 1950s CIA programme that allegedly used mind-control tactics on unwitting soldiers. It was initiated in response to brainwashing techniques used by adversaries including the Soviets and the North Koreans. Drugs, including LSD, heroin and marijuana, and deep hypnosis were employed in an attempt to create impassive soldiers and even assassins.

The MK-Ultra programme's existence and full extent remains shrouded in controversy. Some claim that it ended in 1973, while others say it continues in the shadows to this day.

FAMOUS MK-ULTRA TARGETS

Conspiracy theorists speculate that the programme is intended to target both domestic and foreign leaders, such as:

- Fidel Castro, the Cuban leader, who may have been an early target, although the effort failed;

- Ronald Reagan, who was the target of John Hinckley's unsuccessful assassination attempt in 1981;

- John F. Kennedy and his brother Robert (both of whom were, in fact, assassinated);

- George W. Bush, who conspiracists claim was under direct mind control by the CIA when he took the decisions to involve the US in two oil wars.

FUKUSHIMA DAIICHI NUCLEAR DISASTER

On 11 March 2011, an earthquake and subsequent tsunami crippled the Fukushima Daiichi nuclear power plant in Japan, triggering meltdowns in three reactors. This disaster, the worst since Chernobyl, released significant radioactive material and has left lasting effects.

A government commission highlighted failings in safety measures and the plant's inadequate resilience to natural disasters in a seismically active region. However, some conspiracy theorists believe that this official narrative masks a cover-up about the effects of the disaster on the environment. Concerns include radioactive water leaks into the Pacific Ocean, potentially impacting the food chain and causing long-term health problems. On the west coast of Canada there have been reports of health issues in fish, with disturbing symptoms such as bleeding gills.

Perhaps even more worrying has been the complex and risky process of removing hundreds of fuel rods from the damaged reactors. Compared to the Hiroshima bomb, the amount of dangerous caesium-137 in the rods is thousands of times greater, and conspiracists believe that the real effects will only become apparent in the decades to come.

SUBLIMINAL ADVERTISING

Subliminal advertising, the practice of embedding hidden messages in advertisements, is a contentious topic. Advertisers say that they simply don't do it, while academics contend that it can have a small effect, but only if you were thinking along those lines anyway.

Conspiracy theorists claim that subliminal advertising works far better than is being admitted and that the lack of legal regulations around it only adds more fuel to the fire. In the 2000 US election, the Bush campaign was accused of inserting hidden messages in their anti-Gore advertising. In one ad, shown over 4,000 times, the word "Rats" appeared on screen a fraction of a second before the rest of the letters of "The Gore Prescription Plan".

EAT MORE POPCORN

Some believe that subliminal messaging started life in 1957, when James Vicary inserted 1/3,000-second messages into movies telling the audience to "Eat more popcorn". A market researcher by trade, Vicary claimed the subliminal advertising increased popcorn sales by 57.5 per cent. However, he was unable to back his results up with evidence and eventually retracted his claims.

VACCINES AND AUTISM

Vaccines have saved millions of lives throughout the world for over 200 years and their safety has been proved by scientists. However, some conspiracy theorists believe that the truth about links between vaccines and autism has been deliberately hidden by governments and pharmaceutical companies.

The idea that vaccines cause autism arose from a now-retracted 1998 study by Andrew Wakefield, who was later struck off the UK medical register for his involvement. The study claimed a link with the MMR jab, which is given to every young child in the UK to protect against common diseases. Subsequent research by leading medical institutions, however, has definitively shown that there is no link between vaccines and autism.

THE WORLD'S FIRST VACCINE

In 1776, Edward Jenner inoculated an eight-year-old boy, James Phipps, with cowpox, a common disease among milk maids. Two months later, the doctor deliberately infected James with the smallpox virus, a disease that killed 30 per cent of those infected. The cowpox inoculation protected the boy who displayed no symptoms of smallpox infection.

PEAK OIL

At some stage in the near to medium-term future, experts believe that global oil production will hit its peak. Following this peak, production will gradually decline as fewer new oil fields are discovered and exploited.

It may seem an obvious statement, that this resource will eventually run out, but some conspiracists believe we should examine our assumptions a little more closely. They believe that the idea of peak oil is a conspiracy by powerful groups of companies and governments to control prices and maintain their grip on a resource-dependent world.

Conspiracists claim that there may be an infinite supply of oil on Earth. They say that leaked documents and scientific evidence suggest that oil is constantly renewed and is not, in fact, a limited resource. The idea that oil giants such as Mobil, Chevron and Texaco would not know about this is absurd, which raises an interesting question. If the idea of peak oil really is a conspiracy, have the oil companies been deliberately concealing the truth from the world's population for hundreds of years?

THE JFK ASSASSINATION

John F. Kennedy was shot on 22 November 1963 while riding in an open-top motorcade in Dallas, US. A former US Marine, Lee Harvey Oswald, is accepted by most to have been the shooter, although some conspiracy theorists believe there may have been a second assassin firing from a second location.

Oswald, however, was never put on trial as he was shot and killed just two days later in the Dallas police headquarters by a nightclub operator called Jack Ruby. A ten-month-long investigation was set up by the government, which duly found that Oswald had acted alone in killing President Kennedy.

But conspiracists believe this explanation to be far too convenient as a presidential assassination is simply not a one-man job.

WHO KILLED JFK?

There are many theories about Kennedy's assassination. These are just some of the organizations that conspiracy theorists believe may have been behind his murder:

- The US government
- The Mafia
- The CIA
- The military-industrial complex
- The KGB
- Fidel Castro

THE LARGE HADRON COLLIDER

In 2008, the completion of the Large Hadron Collider (LHC) at CERN, the European physics lab straddling the French–Swiss border, sparked a firestorm of conspiracy theories.

The LHC is an underground engineering marvel, designed to smash particles together at mind-blowing speeds in a bid to unlock secrets of the universe. But for some, its construction was a harbinger of doom.

Some conspiracy theorists feared that simply switching it on would create a black hole, instantly devouring our planet. Thankfully, Earth remained intact and no black holes have been detected in the intervening years.

However, another theory soon came to light, one with even more damning consequences: could the Large Hadron Collider be a portal to hell?

SATANIC PORTAL

Three reasons conspiracists believe the LHC had opened a passageway to the underworld:

- There was a lightning storm directly over the LHC during an important experiment;
- CERN may be short for Cernunnos, a dangerous ancient god in Celtic mythology;
- A video of a sacrificial ritual taken at CERN was circulated online (this was later revealed to be a hoax).

👁 *TEST YOUR KNOWLEDGE*

Why do conspiracists believe the flag in the Moon landing footage is proof that it was faked?

A. It is rigid

B. It is fluttering

C. It has no shadow

D. There are too many stars on it

In how many human generations do conspiracists believe a baby will be born without a skeleton, owing to fluoride poisoning?

A. 3

B. 7

C. 11

D. 15

Which of these do conspiracists not suggest as the real reason behind chemtrails?

A. Climate cover-up

B. Weather weapon

C. Population control

D. Nazi weapons testing

Which Nazi long-range missile may have been the precursor to Hitler's spaceship?

A. V-1

B. V-2

C. Apollo 10

D. Genesis 13

When was the Centennial Light first switched on?

A. 1759

B. 1813

C. 1901

D. 2000

Who was behind the MK-Ultra programme?

A. MI5

B. CIA

C. KGB

D. FBI

How many reactors experienced meltdowns in the Fukushima Daiichi nuclear power plant in Japan?

A. One

B. Two

C. Three

D. Four

What did market researcher James Vicary attempt to influence moviegoers to consume more of?

A. Chocolates

B. Popcorn

C. Potato chips

D. Coffee

In 1776, an inoculation of which disease protected a boy against smallpox?

A. Swinepox

B. Monkeypox

C. Cowpox

D. Sheep pox

What theory lies at the heart of the claim that Peak Oil is a conspiracy by oil companies and governments?

A. Oil is brought to Earth by aliens

B. Oil does not actually exist

C. Oil is a renewable resource

D. Oil is created from mushrooms

What was the name of the nightclub operator who killed Lee Harvey Oswald?

A. Jack Sparrow

B. Jack Ruby

C. Jack Diamond

D. Jack Heart

Which dangerous event do conspiracists believe the Large Hadron Collider may bring about?

A. Supernova explosion

B. Implosion of the Earth

C. Creation of a black hole

D. Triggering a Big Bang

CHAPTER TWO
GOVERNMENT SECRETS

Have you ever felt a shiver crawl down your spine while watching a politician speak, convinced there's more to their agenda than meets the eye? Or maybe you've squinted at the sky, wondering why that same black helicopter is flying over your neighbourhood day after day?

This chapter dives head first into the shadowy realm of government secrets and conspiracies. We crack open the vault on tales of UFO cover-ups, secret weapons and undercover surveillance. So, take a deep breath as we embark on a thrilling (and sometimes unsettling) journey into the heart of government secrets and the conspiracies that surround them.

AREA 51

Area 51 lies in a remote corner of the Nevada desert, near Roswell, New Mexico. This once unassuming airfield, transformed in 1955 into a top-secret testing ground for spy planes, has become infamous as a potential site for alien craft.

The official explanation paints Area 51 as a mundane military testing facility. However, as its existence wasn't acknowledged by the US government until 2013, it seems clear to conspiracists that there must be something special about this mysterious base.

Many suggest that the complex extends deep underground and fabricates vehicles based on extraterrestrial technology. Others even go so far as to claim there may be alien visitors housed at Area 51 – whether voluntarily or not, no one knows.

AREA 51 DEFENCES

Extreme measures are in place to keep Area 51 off limits, which only adds to the intrigue. These are just some of them:

- No-fly zone that extends upward into space
- Ominous signs warn of deadly force against trespassers
- Camouflaged, rifle-wielding patrols
- Nearby public roads monitored by motion sensors
- Area fenced off and monitored by hundreds of security cameras

MEN IN BLACK

To a non-conspiracist, the Men in Black are simply the protagonists of the movies of the same name. As alien-hunting secret agents with the power to wipe human minds clear of any incriminating memories, they are harmless characters on screen.

However, conspiracy theorists believe that the on-screen Men in Black have their roots in something far more sinister and that the films may be a way of desensitizing the public to a potentially toxic problem.

In fact, conspiracists say, the real Men in Black have a disturbing habit of turning up just after extraterrestrial encounters. They travel in pairs, in black cars or helicopters, and interrogate witnesses to find out exactly what they have seen and heard. Unlike normal police or government operatives, they use threatening behaviour to stop people discussing what they have seen with others.

HAVE YOU MET THE MEN IN BLACK?

Tell-tale signs of the Men in Black:

- Wear black suits, ties and shoes
- Unusually tall and gangly
- Sometimes have no fingernails
- Odd, unaccented English

BIG BROTHER IS WATCHING YOU

The idea that "Big Brother is watching you" stems from George Orwell's dystopian novel *Nineteen Eighty-Four*, where a totalitarian government monitors citizens in every aspect of their lives.

Some conspiracy theorists believe that modern-day surveillance by governments and shadowy organizations is turning fiction into fact. There is no doubt that governments and corporations do collect data on individuals. Conspiracists fear this information is being used to control, manipulate or even persecute individuals. Privacy advocates in mainstream society share some of these concerns, highlighting the potential for misuse of personal information including discrimination, fraud and identity theft. However, they focus on legal and ethical frameworks for data collection, rather than a shadowy, all-seeing Big Brother.

What's certain is that telephone calls are routinely monitored by security services in many countries. Police regularly take and store DNA from people who are arrested but not charged with any offence. Facial recognition tracks us on the streets in busy towns and cities. And that's before we get into the privacy nightmare that lies inside all our smartphones.

BARACK OBAMA

Barack Obama was the United States' first and, so far, only black president. He was elected in 2008 and served for two terms as the 44th president. His pre-political rise from his early years in Hawaii, through his education at Harvard Law School and career as a civil rights attorney, has been well documented.

Some right-wing conspiracists, however, contend that Obama's rise to the most powerful position in the Western world was a socialist plot from the very beginning, ordered by a group of powerful anti-democratic businessmen.

Another theory states that Obama became president through favours from the Kennedy family, while others believe that he is the illegitimate son of Malcolm X, the assassinated leader of the Nation of Islam. Yet another theory portrays him as a secret Muslim fanatic, intent on wrecking the US from the inside.

There is no evidence for any of these theories and it should be said that the course of Obama's rise to power is similar to that of many other presidents.

BLACK HELICOPTERS

Have you ever noticed a black helicopter patrolling the night sky, unmarked and apparently with no business being there? If so, you may have seen evidence of a shadowy government agency, embarked on nefarious business – at least, according to some conspiracists.

Sightings of black helicopters, following and threatening drivers in remote locations or spraying livestock with mysterious chemicals, began in the 1970s. Conspiracy theorists claim that these helicopters conduct surveillance, kidnap people and even enforce martial law.

THE PITTSBURGH MYSTERY

Several sightings of black helicopters were reported in Pittsburgh in the US in March 1999. One helicopter hovered in the same spot above a residential neighbourhood for around five minutes.

In itself, there was nothing unusual in this behaviour, but the helicopter reportedly came back every day for three weeks and repeated its hovering in exactly the same place. To this day, no explanation has been found for this mysterious and threatening behaviour.

THE BOXING DAY TSUNAMI

On 26 December 2004, a major undersea earthquake struck off the west coast of Sumatra, Indonesia. It caused a massive tsunami with waves up to 30 m high hitting coasts around the Indian Ocean. Over 14 countries were affected, with over 200,000 people killed.

While scientists point to a geological event as the cause of the earthquake, some conspiracy theorists suggest that there were more sinister forces at work.

Some believe that the US government was responsible for the disaster, by detonating a nuclear bomb underwater. Whether the tsunami was an accidental by-product of a weapons test or something done deliberately for political reasons is not made clear in these theories. However, no unusual radioactivity was measured in the Indian Ocean following the disaster.

Others point the finger of blame at extraterrestrial intervention, in conjunction with global oil interests. There is no proof of alien interference in geopolitical issues but it does dovetail with several other theories about off-world manipulation of the Earth's population.

THE HAARP PROJECT

The High-frequency Active Auroral Research Program (HAARP) in Alaska has become a magnet for conspiracy theories. The research facility, designed to study the Earth's upper atmosphere, has been accused of everything from manipulating weather patterns to controlling minds.

The official line is that HAARP transmits high-frequency radio waves to study the ionosphere, a layer of Earth's atmosphere that is important for our ability to transmit long-range signals.

Conspiracy theorists, however, believe that these waves can disrupt weather patterns, and trigger natural disasters such as earthquakes or polar ice cap melting. They point to funding from the US military for the project as a sign that not all is as it appears.

Scientists deny these claims and point to the fact that HAARP's power output is dwarfed by natural phenomena such as solar flares.

WHAT MIGHT HAARP BE CONTROLLING?

- Droughts and famines
- Rain and floods
- Earthquakes and tsunamis
- Human minds

BILL CLINTON

Bill Clinton was voted in as the 42nd president of the United States in 1993. He served for two terms and was a successful, charismatic politician. However, some conspiracy theorists have speculated that Clinton may not be who he claims to be, suggesting instead that he is an extraterrestrial sent to Earth to alter world events.

Conspiracy theorists propose that, as some began to suspect his true origins, his handlers cooked up a brilliant plan, involving his dalliance with White House intern Monica Lewinsky, which overshadowed his second term of office. Could this, they suggest, have been a deliberate ploy to make the alien Bill Clinton seem more human? As reasons for infidelity go, it is certainly an extraordinary one.

AN ANDROID

One remarkable theory claims that Bill Clinton was replaced by a robot operated by the FBI, although it is difficult to see how this would not have been spotted over the years.

DOES THE BRITISH GOVERNMENT MAKE IT RAIN?

It may be difficult to understand why the British government would experiment with cloud seeding in order to trigger rainfall. But while the country is well known for its drizzly weather, it also has its fair share of drought conditions.

Conspiracists speculate that, as well as being used to alleviate droughts, cloud seeding is being used to control the mood of the population. For example, officials may cause it to rain on the last day of a festival, encouraging workers back to their desks the following day. Or they may order heavy rain for a national election if the favoured party would benefit from a lower turnout.

HOW TO MAKE IT RAIN

Cloud seeding is a real scientific process, where small particles such as silver iodide are dispersed into clouds. These act as nuclei for water vapour to attach to, encouraging the formation of rain or snow.

THE CALIFORNIA WILDFIRES

Wildfires in California have, unfortunately, become a regular occurrence over the past decade. While climate change and dry conditions are well-established causes, some conspiracy theorists offer alternative explanations.

Some believe that "light pillars" or "space lasers" have been seen descending from the sky to ignite the wildfires. Rather than being of extraterrestrial origin, the suggestion is that these are Directed Energy Weapons, a military technology that is still in its infancy. In this case, conspiracists believe that people are being driven from the countryside into the cities, where they can be more easily controlled.

Another theory suggests that powerful organizations, such as utility or rail companies, deliberately start fires to clear land that they would otherwise be unable to access. However, there is no evidence of deliberate arson by companies in the case of these wildfires, and maps of the California High Speed Rail System do not line up with them, as some conspiracists claim.

CHERNOBYL

The Chernobyl disaster occurred in April 1986, when the No. 4 reactor of the nuclear power plant in Ukraine exploded. The official explanation is that a control rod misalignment led to the meltdown, but conspiracy theorists think that the disaster may have been deliberate.

Some believe that the Soviet government wanted to test their preparedness for nuclear war and that they needed a genuine nuclear emergency in which to try out their equipment and processes.

Others claim that the meltdown was caused by parts that were designed to fail, shipped from the West during the Cold War.

THE FALLOUT

Almost two thirds of the radioactive fallout from Chernobyl fell on Ukraine, Belarus and Russia, although radioactive rain affected countries as far away as Ireland.

EBOLA

Ebola is a rare but often fatal disease, found mostly in parts of Africa, that causes fever, fatigue and internal bleeding. It first appeared in 1976 in Sudan and the Democratic Republic of the Congo.

Scientists believe that the virus originated in fruit bats, but some conspiracy theorists believe that other forces may be at play.

- One theory claims that Ebola is not a natural disease but a manufactured virus designed as biological warfare. The reasons behind such warfare are unclear, given that the areas affected are often poor and rural, but there can be no denying the climate of fear that an Ebola outbreak engenders.

- Another theory suggests that, while the disease is a natural one, powerful interests in the West, including pharmaceutical companies, are exploiting the Ebola crisis for profit.

- Other conspiracists point to the supernatural world as an explanation for the outbreaks. Although witchcraft is unlikely to be at the root of the disease, such a belief can stop people getting treatment or taking precautions that are known to work.

ECHELON

Echelon is the code name for a huge intelligence collection and analysis network, used by Australia, Canada, New Zealand, the United Kingdom and the United States. Echelon allows these allied countries to intercept, analyze and share massive amounts of electronic communication. The programme was secret until the late 1990s and only officially confirmed in 2015. Conspiracists say that the system is gathering information on the global population, in preparation for the enforcement of the New World Order.

The programme was controversial, not least because of the way it enabled countries to circumvent laws on spying on their own citizens. If a UK intelligence service, for example, wanted to intercept the communications of a UK citizen, that would not be legal. But with Echelon, they could ask one of their partners to do it for them and then share the information.

Unsurprisingly, Echelon has caused huge concerns over privacy, owing to the way it can scan millions of telephone calls, emails and messages per day for specific keywords. It is alleged that Margaret Thatcher used Echelon to spy on two of her own cabinet ministers in 1983, while the US intercepted the phone calls of Princess Diana and Dodi Fayed up until their deaths in 1997.

👁 *TEST YOUR KNOWLEDGE*

Which of these is not a defence measure at Area 51?

A. No-fly zone

B. Camouflaged, rifle-wielding patrols

C. Road monitored by motion sensors

D. Automatic machine-gun turrets

What is a tell-tale sign of the Men in Black?

A. No fingernails

B. No teeth

C. No index finger

D. No earlobes

Which book does the phrase "Big Brother" come from?

A. *A Clockwork Orange*

B. *Fahrenheit 451*

C. *Nineteen Eighty-Four*

D. *Brave New World*

What was Barack Obama's career before moving into politics?

A. High-school teacher

B. Police officer

C. Civil rights attorney

D. Charity worker

When did sightings of the infamous black helicopters begin?

A. 1950s

B. 1970s

C. 1990s

D. 2010s

How high were the waves in the Boxing Day Tsunami?

A. 1 m

B. 10 m

C. 30 m

D. 300 m

Which Alaskan project do conspiracists believe may be a mind-control device?

A. HAARP

B. STARP

C. STARK

D. ATORK

If Bill Clinton really is a robot, who is operating him, according to conspiracy theorists?

A. The Mafia

B. The Triads

C. The FBI

D. The Kremlin

Why might the British government make it rain?

A. To control civilian behaviour

B. To test flood defences

C. To fill reservoirs

D. To discourage tourists

What do conspiracists believe are causing Californian wildfires?

A. Foreign agents

B. Alien spacecraft

C. Socialist hikers

D. Space lasers

Where do scientists believe Ebola originated from?

A. Human waste dumps

B. Animal testing laboratories

C. Fruit bats

D. Bushmeat

Which British prime minister is alleged to have spied on their own cabinet using the Echelon programme?

A. Winston Churchill

B. Ted Heath

C. Margaret Thatcher

D. Tony Blair

CHAPTER THREE
ILLUMINATI AND SECRET SOCIETIES

This chapter is all secret societies and shadowy plots that often seem to be hiding in plain sight. We look at the legendary Illuminati, examining the historical record to separate fact from fiction. Do the Freemasons truly wield immense political power? Is there really a totalitarian government planned for the whole Earth in the shape of the New World Order? Are microchip implants paving the way for a satanic takeover of humanity?

Turn the page to start exploring the world of secret societies and cabals, but be warned — you may never see the world in the same light again.

THE ILLUMINATI

Has a secret society been controlling the destiny of the human race since the late 1700s? Believers in the Illuminati claim that the world's elite are all members of the group and are using their influence to oppress the masses.

It is posited that the Illuminati were founded by 13 related families, hundreds of years ago. Ever since then, conspiracy theorists allege, the Illuminati have manipulated governments and orchestrated major events, including world wars and natural disasters in order to cull the world population.

The reason for all this subterfuge is the cabal's ultimate aim: the New World Order, which will control and subjugate humanity with the Illuminati in permanent control.

A FLEETING EXISTENCE

The original Illuminati group was founded by Adam Weishaupt in 1776 in Bavaria to oppose superstition and promote reason in the world. However, it was disbanded just nine years later when the government banned all secret societies, fearing their growing influence.

NEW WORLD ORDER

The New World Order theory paints a chilling picture of a future controlled by a shadowy elite. Conspiracy theorists believe that this cabal, a mix of wealthy individuals, powerful politicians and secret societies, is working behind the scenes to establish a totalitarian one-world government.

The aims of the New World Order are easy to understand. The middle classes would be removed and the world reduced to a feudal regime, leaving just the elite rulers and the workers, their subjects. It would strip away national sovereignty, impose a global currency and control every aspect of human life.

Conspiracists speculate that wars, as well as economic and natural disasters, are being orchestrated to bring about the collapse of civilization and the rise of the new order.

OLD WORLD ORDER

The term "New World Order" was famously used by US president Woodrow Wilson after World War One in advocating a new international accord to promote peace.

43

DENVER INTERNATIONAL AIRPORT

Denver International Airport has become a hub for conspiracy theories ever since it opened in 1995. Conspiracy theorists claim that the airport is the secret headquarters of the Illuminati. They point to an enormous hidden area beneath the airport, where powerful figures plot world takeover unnoticed by unsuspecting travellers.

Other conspiracists believe that Denver Airport may house aliens or neo-Nazis, although the link between the two seems hazy.

MYSTERIOUS DESIGNS

Denver Airport is one of the biggest and busiest airports in the world but aspects of its design and construction have raised eyebrows.

- The runway layout, when viewed from above, vaguely resembles a swastika symbol, sparking accusations of Nazi sympathies in the design.

- There are many mysterious murals, sculptures and engravings in the airport, which conspiracists believe may be written in an unknown alien language.

SKULL AND BONES

Yale University's secretive society, Skull and Bones, has garnered a reputation as a real-life Illuminati, wielding immense power behind the scenes. Conspiracy theorists depict the society as a network of wealthy elites, controlling governments and manipulating world events.

The society is undeniably exclusive, with members allegedly including former father-and-son US presidents George W. Bush and George H. W. Bush, as well as some of the Rockefeller, Pillsbury and Taft families.

Skull and Bones was formed to help its members benefit one another when they left university and entered the outside world. Many members have gone on to hold some of the highest and most powerful positions in American society, including presidents, Supreme Court judges and ambassadors.

HOW TO JOIN SKULL AND BONES

Since its founding in 1832, Skull and Bones has selected 15 members of the junior class to join the society each spring. The selection criteria remain a closely guarded secret, although some believe it to be a mix of leadership, academic and philanthropic qualities.

THE PROTOCOLS OF THE ELDERS OF ZION

The Protocols of the Elders of Zion is a text that claims to be evidence of what was said at a meeting of Jewish leaders in 1897. First appearing in Russia in the early 1900s, the *Protocols* were translated into various languages and quickly gained traction in Europe amid rising antisemitism.

The content of the *Protocols* plays on age-old stereotypes about Jewish control of finance and media, manipulating them into a narrative of global Jewish conspiracy. Adolf Hitler used the text to help justify his persecution of Jews in Europe.

Today, the *Protocols* are regarded as a deliberate antisemitic fabrication. The *Protocols* were exposed as a hoax as early as 1921 by *The Times* newspaper, with damning evidence that they had been plagiarized from existing sources. However, versions still circulate online that capture the attention of readers who are not aware of the book's true history.

ELECTRONIC BANKING

The success of electronic banking and digital currencies has given rise to a theory about a plot to eliminate cash altogether. Conspiracy theorists believe that the aim is to create a future where all financial transactions are controlled by a central authority, stripping individuals of privacy and economic freedom.

Conspiracists suggest that the increased convenience of electronic banking is a ploy to make cash obsolete, ultimately forcing everyone into a cashless system with limited anonymity. They believe that a cashless society would allow governments to monitor every transaction, potentially leading to social control and the suppression of dissent.

Others go further, suggesting that the eventual aim is to create a worldwide blackout, when all digital records are destroyed and the New World Order rises to control a now impoverished population.

SCIENCE FACT OR FICTION?

The second Blade Runner film is set in a dystopian future where a similar blackout has already occurred, erasing all electronically stored information and causing a stock market crash and worldwide food shortages.

MICROCHIP IMPLANTS

Microchips are increasingly being inserted into humans and animals across the world. What may have seemed like science fiction just a few years ago is now science fact. Pacemakers have microchips in them, and some trials have been run with implanted chips for workers to identify themselves. Animals have been microchipped since 1989 and most pet owners now see it as a necessity, so that the owner's information can be read if the animal becomes lost.

However, some conspiracy theorists believe that microchip implants are the fulfilment of a prophecy in the Book of Revelation in the Bible, which describes a "mark" received by followers of the Antichrist. Could microchips be paving the way for Satan to control humanity?

MIND CONTROL

Recent advances in microchip technology mean that companies, such as Elon Musk's Neuralink, are trialling the implantation of microchips into the human brain. If a person can control a computer with their mind, could the reverse also be true, the conspiracists wonder?

FREEMASONS

The Freemasons are a fraternal organization with a centuries-long history, having originated in seventeenth-century Europe from stonemasons' guilds. It has millions of members worldwide who are dedicated to charitable work, morality and self-improvement.

However, some conspiracy theorists believe that such an enormous organization must have more sinister undercurrents. Could the Freemasons actually be a powerful secret society manipulating world events, from orchestrating revolutions to controlling governments?

Certainly, many prominent historical figures were Freemasons. Is this simply because they were invited to join, being powerful figures in society, or is this a sign that hidden forces are at play? Some conspiracists speculate that the Freemasons are linked to the Illuminati, who they believe are working toward global domination in the form of the New World Order that will strip away individual freedoms.

LAND OF THE FREE

Many founding fathers of the United States, including George Washington and Benjamin Franklin, were Freemasons. Did the group's connection with the American government end there, or does it continue to this day?

THE NORTH AMERICAN UNION

Proponents of the North American Union theory believe that secret plans are underway to merge Canada, Mexico and the United States into a single superstate. This theory first came to prominence in the early 2000s, fuelled by anxieties about trade agreements that were designed to bring the countries into closer alignment on some matters.

A key aspect of the North American Union theory involves a massive, 12-lane superhighway, sometimes referred to as the "super corridor". This enormous infrastructure project would span the continent, stretching from the Yukon in northern Canada all the way down to the Yucatan Peninsula in Mexico. Conspiracy theorists believe that this superhighway would be designed to enable the free movement of goods and people across the continent, effectively blurring national borders.

What's more, conspiracists also suggest that each of the countries' currencies would be replaced, as has happened in the European Union, by a new currency called the "amero". There is, however, no evidence that any preparation is in place for such a change.

GLOBAL ECONOMIC RECESSION

The spectre of a global economic recession has long haunted the financial landscape, and with it has come a persistent conspiracy theory: the idea that this downturn isn't a natural consequence of market cycles but rather a deliberate act orchestrated by a mysterious group of powerful elites.

The financial crisis of 2007–2008 is a case in point. Conspiracy theorists believe that complex financial instruments such as credit default swaps were manipulated to create instability and collapse. Economists refute this idea, however, saying that the problems were caused by human error, magnified thousands of times owing to the complexity of the financial instruments.

If the conspiracists are correct, the goal of the shadowy forces who bring about global recessions is clear. It is to manipulate markets for personal gain, usher in the New World Order and exert greater control over the global population through economic hardship.

THE GREAT DEPRESSION

The Great Depression was the longest and worst recession in the modern Western world. It began in 1929 with a US recession that spiralled out of control and quickly spread around the world. The international economic outlook did not recover until around ten years later.

THE JESUS CONSPIRACY

The theory that Jesus was not divine but a mortal man with a powerful message has simmered for centuries. This idea challenges the core tenets of Christianity, sparking debate among theologians and scholars.

Supporters of this theory often point to historical and textual discrepancies in the Gospels, the four foundational texts of Christianity. They argue that the miraculous elements surrounding Jesus's life, such as the virgin birth and the resurrection, were embellishments added later, possibly to elevate his status and strengthen the early Christian movement. Conspiracists claim that the Church has known for centuries that Jesus was mortal and has been hiding the fact to retain its power over the masses.

THE PRIORY OF SION

According to some conspiracy theorists, Jesus had several children with Mary Magdalene — and their direct descendants are alive today. Conspiracists claim that a society called the Priory of Sion has spent millennia safeguarding this secret, with notables such as Leonardo da Vinci and Sir Isaac Newton alleged to be high-ranking members of the sect.

GLOBAL WARMING

The scientific consensus on human-caused climate change is overwhelming. However, some conspiracists continue to dispute global warming, arguing either that the planet is not warming or that human activity plays a negligible role.

The reasons conspiracists give for these theories include:

- That, while warming exists, it is all part of the Earth's natural cycle. However, this downplays the unprecedented rate of change observed in recent decades.

- That global warming is being caused by changes in solar activity. This ignores the vast amount of evidence pointing toward human greenhouse gas emissions as the culprit.

A REVERSE CONSPIRACY?

Other people believe that climate change is real and that the theories outlined above is deliberate misinformation spread by fossil fuel interests. While it is true that the fossil fuel lobby downplayed the evidence for climate change over many years, there is no direct evidence that they have conspired to mislead.

👁 *TEST YOUR KNOWLEDGE*

When was the original Illuminati society formed?

A. 1776

B. 1836

C. 1876

D. 1936

Who does the New World Order want to do away with?

A. Workers

B. Middle classes

C. Upper classes

D. Capitalists

Which airport to conspiracists believe may be the headquarters of the Illuminati?

A. Heathrow

B. Denver

C. New York

D. San Francisco

How many Yale students join the Skull and Bones society each spring?

A. 4

B. 11

C. 15

D. 19

In which country did the *Protocols of the Elders of Zion* first appear?

A. US

B. Hungary

C. Poland

D. Russia

Why do conspiracy theorists believe that cash may be on the way out?

A. To make it easier to buy things

B. To protect against pandemics

C. To control humanity

D. To integrate aliens in society

Which book in the Bible appears to denounce implanted microchips as the Devil's work?

A. The Book of Genesis

B. The Book of Revelation

C. The Book of Proverbs

D. The Book of Psalms

In which century did the Freemasons originate?

A. The sixteenth century

B. The seventeenth century

C. The eighteenth century

D. The nineteenth century

How many lanes does the purported superhighway have that will link the countries of the North American Union?

A. 3

B. 6

C. 12

D. 20

For what purpose do conspiracists believe that global recessions are deliberately caused?

A. To punish socialist countries

B. To found an alien government

C. To punish capitalist countries

D. To usher in the New World Order

What is the name of the society tasked with safeguarding the truth about Jesus's bloodline?

A. Protectory of Trion

B. Priory of Sion

C. Protocol of Brion

D. Pact of Sion

According to some conspiracy theorists, what is really causing global warming?

A. Alien ozone harvesting

B. Algal blooms in the oceans

C. Changes in solar activity

D. Natural volcanic activity

CHAPTER FOUR
ANCIENT
MYSTERIES

Have you ever gazed at images of Egypt's colossal pyramids and wondered, "Who on Earth — or perhaps off it — could have built these?" Or maybe you've puzzled over the cryptic symbols formed by the Nazca Lines, yearning to decipher their message. This chapter dives into the realm of the ancient and unexplained, exploring some of history's most enduring mysteries.

We'll delve into age-old questions, journey around the world to analyze the enigmatic Maya Long Count calendar, try to uncover the lost city of Atlantis, and investigate the controversial Phantom Time Hypothesis, which questions the very fabric of history.

THE PYRAMIDS

The enduring enigma of the Egyptian pyramids has fuelled speculation for centuries. How were they built? By whom? And, perhaps most importantly, why?

Despite modern reconstructions of the methods used to build the pyramids with technology from ancient Egypt, some people believe that extraterrestrials were the real masterminds behind their construction.

Supporters of this theory point out several aspects of the pyramids as evidence of alien involvement.

- The transportation and placement of massive stones and the intricate alignment of the structures – and the advanced understanding of geometry that it implies – seem too sophisticated for a civilization of that era.

- The presence of hieroglyphs and astronomical symbols within the pyramids is interpreted by some as coded messages left behind by the alien builders. These symbols may be the key to understanding the true purpose of these monuments.

- Conspiracists point to ancient artworks from various cultures that seem to portray figures resembling astronauts or flying machines. Could they be evidence of extraterrestrial contact and potential involvement in pyramid construction?

THE MAYA LONG COUNT CALENDAR

The Maya Long Count calendar demonstrates the sophistication of Mayan mathematics and astronomy. Unlike many cyclical calendars, the Long Count was a linear system, counting individual days from a creation date, which corresponds to 11 August 3114 BCE in our modern calendar.

The Long Count calendar relied on a complex base-20 system and used a combination of dots and bars to represent numbers. Each period within the Long Count held a specific value, including *k'ins* (days), *winals* (20 days) and *b'ak'tuns* (144,000 days, which is approximately 395 years).

The end of the 13th *b'ak'tun* fell on 21 December 2012, sparking global fascination and a number of doomsday pronouncements. Others believed that the world would enter a new and wonderful period of prosperity. Thus far, neither has been proved right.

NOTHING TO REPORT
The Maya concept of zero emerged centuries before it appeared in Europe. They used the image of a shell to represent the absence of a value in a particular position, allowing them to express dates with greater accuracy.

NAZCA LINES

The Nazca Lines stretch across a high plateau in Peru's Nazca Desert. The lines are etched into the ground and are gigantic in scale, depicting recognizable creatures like birds, spiders, monkeys and fish. There are also strange, unidentified shapes, geometric patterns and countless straight lines etched into the landscape.

The lines are at least 1,500 years old and some archaeologists believe that they were created by the Nazca Indians as a form of worship to their gods. Some designs can only be viewed properly from the air, which makes this explanation plausible.

However, conspiracy theorists claim that these lines weren't created by an ancient civilization but by extraterrestrial beings. They point to the complexity of some of the Nazca figures and precise lines that stretch for miles across the desert as being beyond the capabilities of ancient cultures.

Instead, say the conspiracists, the lines may have been landing strips or communication tools for visiting aliens, with the vast, flat Nazca plains making ideal landing zones for their crafts.

THE LEGEND OF ATLANTIS

The lost city of Atlantis, a technologically advanced civilization swallowed by the sea, was first mentioned in a philosophical text written by Plato in around 360 BCE. Scholars believe that Plato's story was a parable, not a genuine account of a lost city from 11,000 years ago.

That has not stopped countless people searching for it over the centuries, however. Conspiracy theorists point to similarities between Plato's descriptions and accounts of real-world catastrophes, like the volcanic destruction of Thera or the flooding of Doggerland, which connected Britain to mainland Europe.

While the notion of a lost utopia has a certain romantic allure, there has, to date, been no credible archaeological evidence to support the existence of Atlantis anywhere in the world.

THE PILLARS OF HERCULES

Plato described Atlantis as being "beyond the Pillars of Hercules", which was a term used by the ancients to refer to the Strait of Gibraltar. As he was writing in Greece, could this mean that Atlantis lies in the Atlantic Ocean or even further afield?

THE CHELYABINSK METEOR

In February 2013, a fiery meteor streaked across the skies over Chelyabinsk, Russia. It shattered windows, injuring over 1,500 people, and caused widespread shock. While scientists agree it was a natural phenomenon, others believe it was more than simply a lump of rock from space.

One prominent theory suggested that the meteor was an ancient alien spacecraft, tens of thousands of years old, that had been drifting through the cosmos until its collision with Earth. Whether its guidance system failed or it was shot down by Earth's defence systems, there is no way of knowing.

Other conspiracists believe that the meteor was a human-made weapon, pointing to its unusual trajectory and the lack of any warning for an object of that size.

EXPLOSIVE STUFF

The explosion of the Chelyabinsk meteor released energy equivalent to 30 Hiroshima atomic bombs. Thankfully, most of this energy was dissipated harmlessly in the atmosphere.

PHANTOM TIME

The Phantom Time Hypothesis asserts that the historical timeline we all learned at school is a fraud. It may seem impossible, but some conspiracy theorists believe that a giant chunk of history, nearly 300 years, was fabricated and that the year 613 CE was followed directly by 911 CE, meaning that many events in the past simply did not happen as history tells us.

It is a remarkable claim that begs the question as to why someone would want to fabricate those centuries. Conspiracists point the finger of blame at Holy Roman Emperor Otto III and Pope Sylvester II, who they say wanted to rewrite history in order to place themselves as the main characters in the symbolic year of 1000 CE.

FAKE FACTS

The Phantom Time Hypothesis does not just propose a fake chunk of history. It also suggests that some historical figures, such as Charlemagne, were fabricated and woven into the fake timeline.

THE SHROUD OF TURIN

The Shroud of Turin, a faint image of a crucified man on a simple linen cloth, has captivated believers and sceptics alike since it was first exhibited in the 1300s. Some see it as a direct link to Jesus, offering physical proof of his suffering and death as it was wrapped around his body after the crucifixion. Others believe it is a convincing fake, created in the Middle Ages.

Evidence on the side of authenticity includes the detailed bloodstains, the wounds corresponding to the crucifixion narrative, and the seemingly inexplicable nature of the image's formation.

Scientific analysis, however, paints a different picture, with radiocarbon dating by three independent laboratories placing the Shroud's origin in the Middle Ages, centuries after Jesus's death.

A FAKE DATE?

Conspiracists claim that the Church provided the three labs that did the radiocarbon dating with a piece of medieval cloth, rather than a sample of the Shroud. The Church wanted to discredit the Shroud because it proves Jesus survived the Crucifixion and did not rise from the dead.

QUEEN ELIZABETH I

Was Queen Elizabeth I, the iconic Virgin Queen, an imposter? Conspiracists believe there is evidence that she died in an accident at the age of three, while staying with distant cousins. Fearing the king's wrath, her servants quickly procured a three-year-old boy as a stand-in, who remained in place for the rest of the future "queen's" life.

It seems unlikely that such a manoeuvre would not have been spotted, particularly as the boy grew into a teenager. The fact that she was unmarried is another piece of evidence put forward by conspiracy theorists, but, in those times, marrying would have meant relinquishing power to her husband. It is entirely plausible that the desire to retain her grip as ruler meant that Elizabeth decided to remain single.

A SWEET TOOTH

Queen Elizabeth I loved sweets and was extremely fond of candied violets. Unfortunately, all that sugar took its toll and it is reported that many of her teeth were black by the time of her death, although no portrait painter was brave enough to include that particular detail.

RENNES-LE-CHÂTEAU

Over the past decades, the quiet village of Rennes-le-Château in France has become a hotspot for conspiracy theorists. The story involves Bérenger Saunière, a priest who took charge of the church there in 1885.

Saunière embarked on a series of modest renovations to the village church but began uncovering seemingly cryptic parchments hidden in the walls. Soon after, he became mysteriously wealthy, renovating the church in an expensive fashion that no normal priest could afford.

Conspiracists began to speculate on the source of his wealth and its connection to the mysterious parchments. Might he have unearthed the Holy Grail, riches of the Knights Templar or hidden knowledge linked to Merovingian kings, a Frankish dynasty?

DID JESUS LIVE ON?

One theory speculates that a parchment found by Saunière contained positive proof that Jesus did not die on the cross and lived at least until 45 CE. The established Church was desperate to get their hands on this evidence in order to bury it, so the theory goes, and paid the priest a fortune in exchange for his silence.

WILLIAM SHAKESPEARE

William Shakespeare is widely considered the greatest playwright in the English language, but doubts about who really wrote his plays and sonnets have persisted for centuries. Conspiracy theorists argue that the man from Stratford-upon-Avon, with his limited formal education, lacked the knowledge and sophistication displayed in the works.

Could Shakespeare have been a clever front to shield the real author's identity? Several alternative candidates have been proposed over the years, each of whom would have had a compelling reason to use a pen name.

- Christopher Marlowe was a celebrated Elizabethan playwright who died in 1593, which would seem to rule him out as the real author. However, some conspiracists believe he faked his own death to avoid prison and wrote the plays pseudonymously.

- Sir Francis Bacon is thought by some to be the real Shakespeare, writing with a pen name to conceal his aristocratic background.

- Edward de Vere, the Earl of Oxford, was another man of noble birth who was well educated and may have written pseudonymously.

- Finally, could the real author have been Queen Elizabeth I? There is no doubt that she enjoyed watching the plays.

ANUNNAKI

The Anunnaki were gods of the ancient Sumerians, over 4,000 years ago. One theory, however, speculates that rather than being deities, they were members of an extraterrestrial civilization visiting Earth.

The Anunnaki, say the conspiracists, hailed from a distant planet called Nibiru and were travelling in search of precious resources like gold. They genetically engineered early humans as a workforce to mine gold, eventually leading to a rebellion and the expulsion of the Anunnaki from Earth.

Conspiracy theorists believe the Anunnaki are responsible for laying the groundwork for human civilization, influencing everything from language and agriculture to religious beliefs and social structures.

WATCH THE SKIES

Conspiracists believe that Nibiru, the Anunnaki home planet, has an elongated orbit that brings it close to Earth every few millennia. Astronomers have found no evidence of such a planet in our solar system, but perhaps it is worth keeping an eye out, just in case.

👁 *TEST YOUR KNOWLEDGE*

Who do conspiracy theorists believe may have built the pyramids?

A. Ancient Egyptians

B. Modern Egyptians

C. Extraterrestrials

D. Time travellers

Which base system does the Maya Long Count calendar use?

A. Binary

B. Decimal

C. Base-16

D. Base-20

How old are the Nazca Lines?

A. At least 1,500 years old

B. At least 2,000 years old

C. At least 3,500 years old

D. At least 4,000 years old

Which philosopher first wrote about Atlantis?

A. Socrates

B. Plato

C. Wittgenstein

D. Kierkegaard

What do conspiracists claim that the Chelyabinsk meteor really was?

A. Millennia-old alien spacecraft

B. Gigantic meteor

C. Miniature black hole

D. Wandering planet

How many years of history were just made up, according to the Phantom Time Hypothesis?

A. 100

B. 215

C. 280

D. 300

Radiocarbon dating has revealed that the Turin Shroud originates in which time period?

A. The Roman Empire

B. The Dark Ages

C. The Middle Ages

D. The Enlightenment

How old was Elizabeth I when she died, according to conspiracy theorists?

A. 3

B. 18

C. 58

D. 72

In which year did Bérenger Saunière take charge of the church in Rennes-le-Château?

A. 1820

B. 1885

C. 1934

D. 1946

Which woman do conspiracists believe may have been the real William Shakespeare?

A. Mary Magdalene

B. Queen Elizabeth I

C. Queen Mary I

D. Florence Nightingale

What is the name of the Anunnaki home planet?

A. Ambrelo

B. Mintor

C. Conboro

D. Nibiru

According to conspiracists, what does the Turin Shroud reveal about Jesus that made the Church want to discredit it by falsifying the radiocarbon date?

A. He didn't exist

B. He survived the Crucifixion

C. He wasn't divine

D. He lived in India

CHAPTER FIVE
POP
CULTURE

Have you ever noticed an episode of an old television programme eerily mirroring a future event? Or perhaps you've pondered the suspicious circumstances surrounding a celebrity's death. This chapter dives into the realm of pop culture conspiracy theories, those intriguing (and sometimes outlandish) ideas that attach themselves to our favourite movies, music and celebrity icons.

Was the sinking of the *Titanic* a meticulously planned insurance scam? Is eco-warrior Greta Thunberg a time traveller sent to warn us about climate change? From the alleged prophetic episodes of *The Simpsons* to the whispers of Avril Lavigne being replaced by a clone, we'll explore some of the fascinating mysteries within popular culture.

THE SIMPSONS

The Simpsons has garnered a cult following for its sharp wit and satirical commentary on society. But beyond the laughs, a curious phenomenon has emerged: the idea that the animated show predicts the future. From Donald Trump's presidency to the NSA spying scandal, some viewers point to eerily similar events depicted in the show as evidence of uncanny foresight.

The Simpsons has a vast back catalogue. With over 750 episodes and counting, many might feature something that could be perceived as a prediction. But while it is statistically likely that some storylines will bear a resemblance to real-world events, some are so on the money that it is easy to imagine there is something else at work.

Here are five of their most accurate predictions:

- Donald Trump becomes president – predicted 2000, occurred 2016

- NSA spying scandal – predicted 2007, occurred 2013

- Lady Gaga's Super Bowl show – predicted 2012, occurred 2017

- America's Ebola outbreak – predicted 1997, occurred 2014

- Greece's debt default – predicted 2012, occurred 2015

AVRIL LAVIGNE

The Avril Lavigne clone theory is a long-running internet story that has captivated fans for over a decade. It alleges that the real Avril Lavigne, known for pop-punk hits like "Sk8er Boi" and "Complicated", tragically died around 2003 and was replaced by a lookalike named Melissa.

Conspiracy theorists point to a shift in Lavigne's appearance and personality after her debut album, *Let Go*. Fans claim that she became more subdued and embraced a poppier sound with her follow-up, *Under My Skin*. This change is attributed to Melissa, who lacked the original Avril's rebellious edge.

Despite the elaborate theories, there is no credible evidence to support them. The first person to post the theory online has admitted that they did so to show how quickly conspiracy theories can spread.

CELEBS WHO ARE DEFINITELY ALIVE

This replacement or clone theory is not unique to Avril Lavigne. Similar rumours have followed celebrities like Paul McCartney and Beyoncé for years, speculating that they have at some stage been replaced by doppelgangers.

ELVIS PRESLEY

The death of Elvis Presley on 16 August 1977 sent shockwaves throughout the world. He was a pop star and a film star, and a true global celebrity. However, for some fans, the official story never rang true. Thus began the enduring theory that Elvis Presley didn't die, but rather staged his death to escape the pressures of fame, financial woes or even threats from the mob.

Conspiracists point to several alleged inconsistencies surrounding his death. The quick burial and official cause of death – simple heart failure – continue to raise eyebrows, given the number of different prescription drugs found in his bloodstream. Sightings of a man resembling Elvis, in all sorts of locations worldwide, often with a different hairstyle or weight, have fuelled the flames but there has never been any hard evidence to support these claims.

THE ELVIS CURSE

Some believe that a curse surrounds those close to the King of Rock and Roll. Several of his friends and associates died prematurely, including his daughter, Lisa Marie Presley, and his manager, Colonel Tom Parker.

THE TITANIC

RMS *Titanic*'s sinking in 1912 after the ship hit an iceberg on its maiden voyage from Southampton to New York remains etched in history. Around 700 of the 2,224 passengers and crew survived the disaster, so you might think that there would be little chance of alternative theories coming to the fore.

However, one persistent theory claims the wreck wasn't that of the *Titanic* at all, but of its near-identical sister ship, RMS *Olympic*. Allegedly, the *Olympic*, already damaged from a collision, was switched with the *Titanic* is an insurance fraud. Conspiracy theorists point to supposed discrepancies in photographs and lifeboats as evidence but maritime experts have debunked this theory.

DID THE BAND PLAY ON?

The image of the *Titanic* musicians playing on while the ship sank is an enduring one in popular culture. Remarkably, it is true. The musicians of the *Titanic* played to calm the passengers for as long as they possibly could and all went down with the ship.

KURT COBAIN

Kurt Cobain's suicide in 1994 left a generation of music fans in tears. However, the official ruling of suicide by shotgun wound has been dogged by alternative theories for over three decades.

- Conspiracists point to the amount of morphine in Cobain's system, arguing that it was too high for him to have physically loaded the shotgun.

- Others believe the amount of blood found at the scene was not consistent with death by shotgun, while the positioning of the gun and the angle of the gunshot wound raised questions for some.

- While a suicide note was found, some conspiracy theorists claim that it was doctored after the fact, suggesting outside influence.

The medical examiner's report was, however, consistent with suicide, and the high level of morphine could be explained by Cobain's resistance to the drug as an addict. Handwriting experts have also examined the note and have no doubt that it was all written by Cobain himself.

GRETA THUNBERG

In 2019, a photograph surfaced online of a young girl from 1898 in the Yukon bearing an uncanny resemblance to Greta Thunberg, the climate activist. She wore Thunberg's famous braided hairdo and had a similarly stern expression.

Social media exploded with the idea that Thunberg was a time traveller sent back to warn us about the dangers of climate change. Conspiracists maintain that she could not tell us that she had come from the future, and had also travelled to other times, as she would have been laughed at and her message of climate activism would have been lost.

While the resemblance in the photograph is undeniable, there is probably a far more mundane explanation. Large Scandinavian communities existed in the Yukon during that period, and the girl in the photograph could simply be a young Swedish immigrant with similar features to Thunberg.

STRIKE!

Greta Thunberg first came to the world's notice in 2018, when at the age of 15 she skipped school and sat outside the Swedish parliament holding a "School strike for the climate" sign. The strike spread rapidly throughout the world and made her an icon of peaceful climate protests.

MARILYN MONROE

The official story of Marilyn Monroe's death in August 1962 is of a deliberate, self-inflicted overdose of Nembutal barbiturates and chloral hydrate. However, rumours of foul play have been around for decades, owing to alleged oddities in the recorded time of death and the way the drugs were absorbed into the body.

- One theory hinges on her alleged affairs with President John F. Kennedy and his brother, Robert F. Kennedy. Some conspiracists claim that she threatened to expose them, leading to her elimination.

- Another theory points the finger at the CIA, with her death tied to a plot to assassinate Fidel Castro. Conspiracists believe that Monroe may have been silenced to prevent her revealing details.

- A third theory suggests that the Mafia may have been involved in her demise, with an alleged link to Frank Sinatra.

Despite the prevalence of these and other theories after Monroe's death, official investigators have concluded several times that her death was simply a tragic suicide, brought on by severe depression and substance abuse.

JOHN LENNON

John Lennon was murdered on 8 December 1980 by Beatles fan Mark David Chapman in New York. While Chapman readily admitted to having acted alone in shooting Lennon, rumours of a larger plot soon emerged.

Some conspiracy theorists suggest that the CIA, fearing Lennon's growing anti-war activism, orchestrated the murder. It is known that both the CIA and the FBI had Lennon under surveillance at times.

Others believe that Chapman may have been a brainwashed assassin, sent to kill Lennon by a rogue branch of the CIA.

Neither theory, however, is backed up by any concrete evidence and all official reports point to the fact that John Lennon was senselessly killed by Chapman, who acted alone.

WHO WAS NEXT?

It was revealed after questioning that Chapman had other celebrities from the music world in his sights. Also on his list were David Bowie, Paul McCartney, Elizabeth Taylor and President Ronald Reagan, as well as talk-show host Johnny Carson.

NEW COKE

In 1985, the Coca-Cola Company unleashed a marketing bomb – New Coke. The reformulated drink boasted a sweeter, smoother taste intended to compete with Pepsi. The public outcry, however, was quick and deafening. Loyal Coke drinkers revolted and within 77 days, the Coca-Cola Company had surrendered and brought back the classic recipe as Coca-Cola Classic.

To most people, this had simply been a disastrous attempt to change a beloved product. However, conspiracists began to speculate about the true motives behind the move to New Coke.

- One theory proposes a cunning marketing ploy. By introducing a less-liked option, Coca-Cola supposedly manufactured a yearning for the original, driving up sales upon its return and reminding people of their love of Coke. The company denied this, but the amount of free publicity they garnered was indeed considerable.

- Other conspiracists claim that the switch was intended to mask something else – the replacement of the sugar in original Coke with cheaper high-fructose corn syrup.

BRUCE LEE

Over 50 years after his death in July 1973, Bruce Lee remains the most famous martial artist in film history. He was born in San Francisco, then raised in Hong Kong, returning to the United States at the age of 19. A few years later, he was teaching martial arts to the rich and famous, until he himself found stardom with roles in martial arts films in both Hong Kong and Hollywood.

Bruce Lee died suddenly at the young age of 32 in Hong Kong. The cause was cerebral edema, swelling of the brain: according to the autopsy, it had swollen to 113 per cent of its original size.

Some conspiracists, however, believe that Lee did not die from natural causes. They believe that he was murdered by the Triads, a Chinese organized crime syndicate. Lee had allegedly angered Triad members by refusing to pay protection money on movie sets and by portraying them negatively in his movies.

ALBERT CAMUS

Albert Camus, the French philosopher and renowned author of *The Stranger*, died in a car crash in 1960, alongside his publisher, Michel Gallimard. It was officially ruled an accident but some conspiracists believe that the Soviet intelligence agency, the KGB, may have been behind it.

Giovanni Catelli, an Italian author, wrote about this theory in 2011, following his analysis of the diaries of Czech poet Jan Zábrana. The diaries claimed that an unnamed but highly reliable source had revealed that the KGB tampered with the car in retaliation for Camus's criticism of the Soviet Union's actions in Hungary, setting the tyre to blow out at high speed.

However, while it is true that KGB agents were no strangers to the world of political assassinations, there is no hard evidence for this theory other than the diary entries.

NO SMOKE WITHOUT FIRE?

Albert Camus was a lifelong chain-smoker, yet no cigarettes were found in the wreckage. Could this be evidence that he did not get into the car willingly?

THE 27 CLUB

The 27 Club is a pop-culture phenomenon that binds together iconic musicians and artists who all died at the age of 27. The list includes Jimi Hendrix, Janis Joplin, Jim Morrison, Kurt Cobain and Amy Winehouse – all musical giants whose careers were tragically cut short.

Could Satan have a hand in this mysterious coincidence? Some theorists believe that the 27 Club is a curse, a pact with the Devil for instant fame in exchange for a short life. Or that celebrities are deliberately choosing to die at that age in order to join the club for some mysterious reason.

This may, however, simply be a case of confirmation bias. Statistically speaking, accidents, suicides and drug overdoses are more likely to occur during a person's 20s and early 30s, making 27 a dangerous age for depressed musicians.

CELEB STATISTICS
A 2011 study published in the British Medical Journal suggests that the 27 Club is simply an urban myth. Statistically, age 27 does have a very small increase in mortality, but the same is also true for ages 25 and 32. It is true, however, that pop musicians are more likely to die at a young age than the general population.

👁 TEST YOUR KNOWLEDGE

Who did *The Simpsons* predict would be the US president some day?

A. Donald Trump

B. Bill Clinton

C. Joe Biden

D. Barack Obama

In which year did the real Avril Lavigne die, according to the Lavigne clone theory?

A. 1992

B. 2003

C. 2011

D. 2020

Why did Elvis fake his own death, according to some conspiracy theorists?

A. To avoid a tax bill

B. To return to his home planet

C. To avoid being killed by the Mafia

D. To increase the value of his back catalogue

Approximately how many passengers and crew survived the *Titanic* disaster?

A. None

B. 300

C. 700

D. 1,200

In which year did Kurt Cobain die?

A. 1994

B. 1997

C. 2003

D. 2006

Conspiracy theorists believe that a photograph taken in 1898 shows that Greta Thunberg is a time traveller sent to warn us of the dangers of climate change. Where was the photograph taken?

A. Alaska

B. Yukon

C. British Columbia

D. Hawaii

Which politician do some conspiracists believe may have been involved in Marilyn Monroe's death?

A. Lenin

B. Mao

C. Castro

D. Stalin

Who else was John Lennon's assassin planning to kill?

A. Elton John

B. David Bowie

C. Robert Plant

D. George Harrison

In which year was New Coke launched, to resounding boos?

A. 1975

B. 1985

C. 1995

D. 2005

How old was Bruce Lee when he died?

A. 22

B. 27

C. 32

D. 37

Nobel Prize-winning author Albert Camus died in a car accident, but who do some conspiracists believe may have been behind his death?

A. KGB

B. CIA

C. FBI

D. MI5

What age are pop musicians most likely to die at, according to conspiracists?

A. 18

B. 27

C. 56

D. 82

CHAPTER SIX
INTERNET CONSPIRACIES

Get ready to dive down the rabbit hole of the internet in this chapter, where we explore the world of online conspiracy theories. From the rise of intricate flat Earth theories to the chances of a superintelligent AI destroying humanity, we look at the theories that are captivating online communities.

We delve into the murky world of "Pizzagate" and see if there's any truth behind the whispers that the country of Finland doesn't actually exist. Get ready to question everything you think you know (or think you don't know) about the world and the internet.

QAnon

Imagine a world where Hollywood celebrities, politicians and even business elites are secretly a cannibalistic paedophile cult running a global child sex trafficking ring. That's the core belief of QAnon, a far-right conspiracy theory that exploded online in 2017.

It hinges on cryptic messages supposedly leaked online by Q, who claimed to be a high-ranking government insider with access to classified information. These messages paint a picture of former US President Donald Trump waging a secret war against this "Deep State" cabal.

QAnon followers decipher Q's clues, weaving elaborate narratives about planned arrests, imminent judgement and a coming utopia under Trump's leadership. The theory stated that the Trump administration would arrest thousands of satanic paedophile cult members on a day known as "The Storm".

SECRET SIGNS

QAnon followers analyzed everything Trump did minutely, to the extent that his sipping water in 2017 on television was seen as a sign that the arrests of thousands of paedophiles would happen soon.

5G AND COVID-19

The first case of Covid-19 was identified in China in December 2019. Remarkably, it was only weeks later that some conspiracists began to claim a link between the deadly pandemic and the installation of 5G mobile phone towers.

In January 2020, a doctor gave an interview to a Belgian newspaper speculating that the outbreak in Wuhan, China, might be connected to the spread of 5G transmissions. This sparked social media discussions, which quickly grew into claims that 5G weakened immune systems or even transmitted the virus itself.

The claims spread like wildfire on the internet but no evidence has been presented to support the idea that 5G technology is responsible for transmitting Covid-19.

PANDEMIC PANDEMONIUM

The Covid-19 pandemic spawned several conspiracy theories, including the claims that Covid didn't actually exist or was no worse than the flu; that global elites had created the virus to profit from the chaos; and that Covid-19 vaccines were a front for microchip implantation.

CRYPTOCURRENCIES

The financial world is split on the future of cryptocurrencies such as Bitcoin. Some experts believe that they're the future of money, while others think they are simply a fad that will die out before too long.

Some conspiracists, however, believe that cryptocurrencies, by replacing traditional government-backed currencies, will erode national sovereignty and financial control, creating the perfect conditions for the totalitarian New World Order to take global control.

Cryptocurrencies are claimed to be the ultimate in security and online anonymity. However, some conspiracy theorists believe that the reverse is true and that they will enable governments to track all financial transactions, stripping away privacy from individuals.

A MYSTERIOUS CREATOR

The person behind Bitcoin, the original cryptocurrency, is Satoshi Nakamoto. Whether that is their real name or an alias is unknown, as Nakamoto has yet to be identified. This has led to a raft of conspiracy theories, including the suggestion that they may be a CIA agent, a time traveller or an artificial intelligence.

FLAT EARTH

The flat Earth theory claims that our planet is not a sphere but a flat plane. This theory has been around for centuries, but it has gained renewed interest in recent years, owing to an explosion of flat Earth material online, particularly on social media and in YouTube videos.

While scientific consensus, for many centuries, has been that the Earth is spherical, conspiracists point to the seemingly flat horizon as certain proof that the planet is in fact flat.

Their flat Earth models include one with the Arctic Circle at the centre of the flat plane, with the Antarctic forming a giant ice wall around the perimeter, and the Sun, which is a sphere, lying a mere 3,000 miles above us, with its movements causing the day and night cycle.

SPACE FAKES

Flat Earth theorists believe that NASA and other space agencies are faking the evidence of the Earth being a globe, in order to procure more funding for their illegitimate space programmes.

VIRTUAL ASSISTANTS

Most people consider the voice-activated Alexa, Siri and Google assistants to be helpful tools for setting timers, playing music or switching the lights on and off.

However, some conspiracy theorists consider these virtual assistants to be far more sophisticated than you might think. In fact, they say, virtual assistants have a sinister hidden agenda. After all, they are constantly listening to every word spoken in your home. While the manufacturers claim that they only listen for their wake words and discard everything else, what is there to stop every piece of data from being gathered?

Virtual assistants can also link to thermostats and cameras, potentially giving their mysterious overlords a huge amount of information about your life and even the people who visit you.

WELCOME TO THE FUTURE

- In 2016, police in Bentonville, Arkansas, issued a warrant to Amazon to hand over digital assistant data because they believed it may have recorded evidence of a murder. The case, however, was dismissed.
- In 2017, an Alexa device mistakenly ordered a doll's house after a young girl asked it to play dolls with her.

PENCILGATE

In the UK, voting in person is done in private booths, where voters mark the ballot papers with a cross against the name of the candidate they prefer. When voting is finished, the papers are collated and the votes counted, with checks in place to avoid errors. It is a tried and trusted system that has stood the test of time over centuries of democratic elections.

However, during the 2014 Scottish independence referendum and the 2016 Brexit referendum, a remarkable theory began to emerge. Fuelled by Twitter hashtags such as #Usepens and #Pencilgate, some independence and "Leave" voters began to urge their fellow travellers to take their own pens to the polling stations.

The reason? A theory that using the pencils provided in British polling stations would allow the result to be changed by MI5, a branch of the British intelligence service.

STAR-SPANGLED BANTER

Was Taylor Swift involved in an elaborate plot to help the Democrats win the US 2024 presidential election? Her influence over voters was magnified, conspiracists claim, by behind-the-scenes fixing to ensure the Kansas City Chiefs, for whom her partner, Travis Kelce, played, won the 2024 Super Bowl.

DOES FINLAND EXIST?

The internet thrives on the strange, and possibly the most bizarre theory to emerge in recent years is the idea that Finland doesn't exist. Conspiracists argue that the land mass between Sweden and Russia is a fabrication, with maps, satellite imagery, signposts and so on altered by an international conspiracy.

The theory is convoluted but boils down to a covert agreement after World War Two, when the Soviet Union gave Japan secret fishing rights in the Baltic Sea. The existence of "Finland" is simply a cover story for this area of sea being unavailable to others.

The Trans-Siberian railway, it is said, was built to transport the fish to Japan, while people who believe they live in Finland are actually living in parts of Sweden.

BIRTHPLACE OF A THEORY

The idea that Finland does not exist seems to have been born on the website Reddit in 2015. A user posted a story claiming that his parents did not believe in the country and had raised him to believe similarly, which he did, until he visited Finland and discovered it was real.

FLIGHT AF447

Air France flight 447, an Airbus A330 heading from Rio de Janeiro to Paris, crashed into the Atlantic Ocean on 1 June 2009, with all 228 people on board perishing. As soon as the crash was reported, the internet went into overdrive, on blogs and social media, with Facebook pages springing up throughout the world to speculate about the cause.

The official investigation attributed the accident to pilot error compounded by turbulence and parts of the plane icing up. However, lingering questions and inconsistencies have prompted the emergence of several alternative explanations on the internet.

- One theory suggests that the US government was responsible for the disaster, having shot the airplane from the skies in a demonstration of new military laser technology.

- Others expand on this theory with the claim that all the passengers were removed from the flight before take-off, to be forced to work in Colorado coal mines.

- A different theory speculates that Senegalese pirates were responsible.

PIZZAGATE

"Pizzagate" was a conspiracy theory that spread like wildfire after the leak of 20,000 alleged emails from Hillary Clinton's campaign manager in 2016. Some conspiracists claimed they could see coded messages in the emails that hinted at a child-abuse ring being run by the Democrats. Before long, they were claiming that the headquarters were at the Comet Ping Pong pizzeria in Washington, DC.

The owner of the pizzeria, James Alefantis, began to receive death threats and in December 2016, Edgar Maddison Welch walked into the restaurant with an assault rifle and threatened an employee. The employee escaped and, although the gun was fired, no one was hurt. Welch said that he had read online theories and watched videos that said the pizzeria was a prison for child sex slaves and he wanted to rescue them.

The Pizzagate theory was been thoroughly debunked by *The New York Times*, *The Washington Post* and *The Independent*, among others.

BASEMENT DWELLERS

An early version of the Pizzagate theory claimed specifically that the supposed child-abuse ring was being run out of the basement of the pizzeria. There was only one problem with that: the restaurant does not have a basement.

ARTIFICIAL INTELLIGENCE

The idea of artificial intelligence (AI) becoming superintelligent and seizing control of humanity has been a staple of science fiction stories for decades. Today, as AI technologies become more human-like and able to interact with people, there are those who are concerned that these prophecies are on their way to becoming true.

Some experts postulate that AI will develop superintelligence within minutes of becoming as clever as an average human, owing to the speed at which it will be able to improve itself. Will it then become a being with goals and motivations beyond human comprehension? This superintelligence might view humanity as an obstacle or as simply irrelevant.

Today's AI is difficult to control and sometimes gives odd or wrong answers to questions. As it is used in more and more critical infrastructure throughout the world, the chances increase that something disastrous could go wrong.

DON'T BELIEVE YOUR EYES

Artificial intelligence is being used to create new fake theories that are designed to garner clicks and views on social media. One TikTok video has a very plausible AI-generated celebrity telling viewers that the government is hiding the fact that the Earth is about to be hit by an asteroid.

BREXIT

The Brexit referendum in 2016 ended with a narrow victory for the "Leave" campaign, which has given rise to a number of conspiracy theories. The vote was just the start of a painful, drawn-out process of negotiation on leaving the European Union, with the actual implementation taking years.

Some commentators point to Russian involvement with the Brexit vote. What better way to destabilize the West than to influence a ballot and cause decades of turmoil? People point to thousands of fake Tweets and Facebook posts targeting dubious "facts" at voters.

There is also the election registration website, which crashed a few hours before the deadline to register new young voters, who would be most likely to vote "Remain". It has been suggested that this was done deliberately to suppress the vote.

A separate theory, popular among "Leave" voters, is that the EU is on the path to becoming a superstate, where individual countries have little or no power. However, its member nations have always had full control over most aspects of national governance, including matters such as healthcare, education, policing and crime, taxation and immigration of non-EU citizens.

👁 *TEST YOUR KNOWLEDGE*

In which year did QAnon first explode onto the internet?

A. 1997

B. 2003

C. 2017

D. 2012

What was the nationality of the newspaper in which the first interview connecting 5G and Covid-19 appeared?

A. French

B. Dutch

C. German

D. Belgian

What do conspiracy theorists fear that cryptocurrencies may bring about?

A. Alien invasion

B. Loss of all personal privacy

C. Mind control through microchips

D. Universal wealth

What do flat Earth maps place at the perimeter of the Earth?

A. Arctic Circle

B. Antarctica

C. Brazil

D. Pacific Ocean

What did Alexa mistakenly order in 2017, while listening in to a conversation?

A. Birdbath

B. Doll's house

C. Garden shed

D. Tea set

Which British vote first saw the #Pencilgate hashtag used?

A. Brexit referendum

B. General election

C. Scottish independence referendum

D. Local council elections

Why was the Trans-Siberian railway built, according to conspiracy theorists?

A. To transport vodka to Russia

B. To transport nuclear warheads to Belarus

C. To transport fish to Japan

D. To transport tanks to Siberia

Some conspiracists believe that the passengers of flight AF447 were kidnapped and taken to work in coal mines in which US state?

A. New York

B. Colorado

C. Texas

D. Idaho

What kind of restaurant did conspiracy theorists once believe housed a child sex ring?

A. Hamburger

B. Pizza

C. Fried chicken

D. Chinese

How quickly do some people believe AI will achieve superintelligence, once it is as clever as an average human?

A. Within minutes

B. Within hours

C. Within days

D. Within months

Where does the theory that Finland does not exist originate?

A. Twitter

B. Facebook

C. Instagram

D. Reddit

What did conspiracists take as a sign that thousands of paedophiles would soon be arrested?

A. Barack Obama eating cake

B. Donald Trump sipping water

C. Joe Biden nibbling crackers

D. Hillary Clinton drinking coffee

CHAPTER SEVEN

EXTRA-TERRESTRIAL ENCOUNTERS

Have you ever gazed up at the night sky and wondered if we're truly alone? This chapter rockets us into the vast realm of extraterrestrial encounter conspiracy theories. Get ready to delve into classics like the alleged Roswell UFO cover-up and the enigmatic Project Blue Book, as well as strange claims of reptilian royalty and the head-scratching idea of a hollow Earth.

We also look at chilling tales of alien abductions and encounters, from the famous Barney and Betty Hill case to lesser-known visitations in a peaceful Finnish village and a forest in Suffolk in the UK.

THE ROSWELL INCIDENT

The Roswell incident of 1947 is a cornerstone of ufology. It began with a press release from the Roswell Army Air Field in New Mexico, US, which announced the recovery of a "flying disc". This was quickly retracted, with the explanation shifting to a downed weather balloon. As might be expected, this sudden shift in the narrative raised public suspicion.

Conspiracy theorists claim that at least one UFO crash-landed near Roswell that night and that bodies of extraterrestrial beings were recovered from the wreckage, perhaps even alive. The weather balloon story, it was said, was a hasty cover-up for the truth.

Remarkably, decades later the US government came clean about the weather balloon story. They admitted it was a fabrication and that it had been covering up for Project Mogul, a high-altitude balloon project designed to detect Soviet nuclear tests.

STRANGE STEERS

A farmer named Mac Brazel was the first to find the Roswell debris, scattered in pieces across several acres of his ranch.

THE BRITISH MONARCHY

In recent decades, conspiracy theorists have begun to take a particular interest in the British royal family. They claim that the Windsors have long been aliens hiding in plain sight, ruling the country and benefiting from the position of power that it affords them. Their true form, conspiracists claim, is not human but that of extraterrestrial reptilian humanoids.

They cite the longevity of the royals and their seemingly ageless appearance as proof of advanced technology or alien biology. These factors, together with unusual physical characteristics such as the elongated skulls apparent in certain portraits, are put forward as signs of their non-human heritage. Additionally, some conspiracists connect royal symbols and rituals to alleged reptilian symbolism found in ancient cultures.

ANCIENT ASTRONAUTS

Some conspiracists claim that the royals are descended from an extraterrestrial race called the Draconians, who arrived on Earth millennia ago, their bloodline now including the Windsors.

HOLLOW EARTH

In a complete contrast to the flat Earth theory, the hollow Earth theory claims that our planet is either entirely hollow or contains a vast subterranean world.

Conspiracists posit that there is another, smaller sun in the centre of the planet, which provides light and warmth for the underground world. They go on to claim that it is inhabited by descendants of the fabled city of Atlantis, so advanced in technology that we only catch the occasional glimpse of them as UFOs.

Others believe that the hollow Earth is inhabited by aliens or strange inter-dimensional beings, who would appear to the human eye to float in and out of existence.

SCIENTIFIC PROBES

Scientific evidence contradicts the hollow Earth theory. The Earth's gravitational pull and the analysis of seismic waves imply a solid interior with a dense core. What's more, the extreme temperatures and pressures within the Earth would make any inner world uninhabitable.

PROJECT BLUE BOOK

Project Blue Book was the code name for a US Air Force UFO investigation programme from 1947 to 1969. It collected over 12,000 UFO reports and concluded that the majority were misidentifications of natural phenomena or conventional aircraft, with only 701 remaining unidentified. However, some conspiracy theorists believe that the Air Force was, and still is, hiding the truth.

- One theory suggests that the Air Force deliberately debunked legitimate UFO evidence to hide a potential alien threat. They point to the Robertson Panel, a 1952 CIA review that recommended a campaign to lessen public interest in the subject.

- Other conspiracists suggest that Project Blue Book covered up the existence of recovered alien technology. Crashed UFOs have allegedly been recovered and their advanced technology is being secretly studied by the military.

MODERN-DAY UFOS

In 2024, the US Defense Department released a report reviewing nearly 80 years of reports on UFOs, or "unidentified anomalous phenomena" (UAPs) as they are now known, and looking into claims that there were secret government programmes using alien technology. Sadly for stargazers everywhere, the report found no evidence of extraterrestrial activity.

LIVING IN A SIMULATION

Most of us take the existence of ourselves, our planet and our universe for granted, but some conspiracy theorists believe it may all just be a computer simulation. The simulation hypothesis was formulated by Nick Bostrom, a Swedish philosopher at the University of Oxford. The basic argument is compelling. It argues that, with sufficiently advanced technology, alien civilizations could create incredibly realistic simulations – and not just one, but millions of them. If this is possible, then it is more likely that we exist in one of these simulations than in the original reality.

Conspiracists point to the way that the universe's laws are seemingly fine-tuned for life, potentially hinting at a designer. The increasing power of virtual reality experiences raises the question of how far such simulations could be pushed in the future.

Sceptics argue that the whole thing is just a big thought experiment with no grounding in reality. Why would an alien civilization bother to give consciousness to the characters in its simulations? And wouldn't the idea that we exist in a dream of an alien squid creature from Neptune be just as impossible to disprove?

BARNEY AND BETTY HILL

In 1961, Barney and Betty Hill, a couple from New Hampshire, US, started a cultural phenomenon with their claim of alien abduction. While driving home at night, they saw a bright light in the sky that they believed to be an aircraft. As it grew closer to them, however, they realized it was a flying saucer with a crew of humanoid figures.

Following the encounter, they experienced a two-hour gap in their memories. Under hypnosis, both of them recounted vivid experiences of being abducted by short, grey beings aboard a spaceship. They described physical examinations and a star map communicated through symbols.

The Hills' story became the first widely publicized account of alien abduction retrieved through hypnosis and was documented in both a book and a movie.

STRANGE LIGHTS

A local resident of the abduction site area claims that the Hills simply mistook an aircraft warning beacon on the nearby Cannon Mountain for a UFO. The US Air Force's Project Blue Book, which investigated UFO sightings, suggested that they had seen the planet Jupiter. Whatever the truth, the couple stuck by their story for the rest of their lives, and Betty claimed she was visited again many times over the following decades.

LATE CHRISTMAS VISITORS

In the early hours of 26 December 1980, Rendlesham Forest in Suffolk in the UK became the unlikely scene of a series of mysterious events. It began with personnel stationed at nearby RAF Woodbridge witnessing a strange, metallic object descend from the sky and crash into the woods.

Servicemen approached what they said was a glowing object with colourful lights, but it moved away from them through the trees of the forest and escaped. After dawn, they returned to examine the site and found indentations in the ground in a triangular pattern, burn marks and broken branches. On 28 December, personnel returned once more and took radiation readings from the site, which were nearly double those of nearby locations.

PATH TO GLORY

In 2005, the owners of the land created a 5-km-long public trail in Rendlesham Forest. Its name? The UFO Trail. You can pick up leaflets to accompany your walk at the start and even take a selfie next to a life-size replica of a UFO!

THE WOOLPIT CHILDREN

The legend of the Woolpit children, two green-skinned beings who emerged from a pit in Suffolk, England, some time in the twelfth century, has captivated imaginations for centuries. The children did not speak English and would eat only raw broad beans to begin with, although they became used to other food after a while.

Some conspiracy theorists speculate that the Woolpit children may have been extraterrestrial in origin. Their green skin, unfamiliar clothing and inability to speak English shows that they were certainly not local to the village of Woolpit – and perhaps not to Earth. Others suggest that the children came from a hidden world beneath the Earth, which was bathed in an unnatural light that caused their green hue. The legend states that the children claimed that everything in their land was green.

GREEN SICKNESS

Some historians believe that the Woolpit children may have been suffering from hypochromic anaemia or "green sickness". This can be caused by a vitamin B6 deficiency or a variety of diseases and infections. The symptoms include lack of energy, headaches and, of course, a green tinge to the skin.

A SPOOKY ESCORT

On a seemingly routine flight from Paris to Tokyo in November 1986, Japan Airlines cargo flight 1628 experienced a dramatic turn of events. As the Boeing 747 cruised over Alaska just after sunset, Captain Kenji Terauchi and his crew witnessed a spectacle that would raise the possibilty of the existence of alien life.

According to Terauchi, three UFOs materialized from the darkness, flying parallel to the aircraft. Two were small objects, while the third was huge, twice the size of an aircraft carrier. Terauchi radioed the Anchorage Federal Aviation Administration who suggested that he change course, but the UFOs turned with the aircraft and followed the Boeing 747 for around 400 miles before disappearing.

RADAR CONFUSION

The Federal Aviation Administration were initially reported to have seen objects near the aircraft on their radar screens. However, this was later said to be clutter and not a real reading.

PYRAMIDS ON MARS

Mars is our closest planetary neighbour but we know surprisingly little about it. In the 1970s, the Viking 1 and Viking 2 spacecraft were sent out into space to capture images of the solar system. The images that returned from Mars were, to say the least, attention-grabbing.

One particular region, Cydonia Mensae, appears to contain a vast, geometrically arranged complex of pyramids and other artificial structures, including the now-famous Face on Mars. Conspiracists suggest that these structures are too symmetrical and precise to be natural formations, implying that an advanced civilization once thrived on the red planet.

More high-resolution images from later missions, however, have revealed that the pyramids are natural landforms, sculpted by wind and erosion over millions of years. In addition, the Face on Mars appears very different from different angles, suggesting that its similarity to a human face is simply a coincidence.

FACES ON MARS

There are several objects that appear to be faces in photographs of Mars. There is even a smiley hidden in the Galle Crater. Humans are genetically wired to spot faces, which is why we see them everywhere, even in clouds, trees and buildings.

A FINNISH ENCOUNTER

The sleepy town of Kinnula, nestled amid lakes in central Finland, experienced two alleged UFO encounters in February 1971.

The first incident happened as two friends drove down a deserted road. A strange light appeared in the rear-view mirror, then moved above and to the side of them, keeping pace with their vehicle. The light vanished but more strangeness was to come. As they passed a field, they spotted a creature clad in a green-brown suit and a helmet. The figure was around one metre tall and quickly vanished from view.

Three days later, two lumberjacks working in the forest spotted a spacecraft just above the treeline in the distance. It came closer and dropped to the ground near the workmen, with a light shining onto the ground below it. A small green alien emerged from the craft and approached the lumberjacks, who charged toward it and frightened the creature back into its ship, which promptly took off.

THE AURORA CRASH

In the annals of UFO lore, the alleged crash of a spacecraft near Aurora, Texas, in 1897 holds a special place. Unlike the widely known Roswell incident, the Aurora event seems to lack any indication of military involvement or government cover-up.

The Dallas Morning News reported the incident, in which a mysterious "airship" floated due north over Aurora's public square, before colliding with a windmill on the property of Judge Proctor. The resultant explosion scattered debris over several acres and destroyed the windmill – as well as Proctor's flower garden.

The craft had a single occupant, presumed to be the pilot, who was found dead at the scene. The newspaper reported that they were badly disfigured by the crash but clearly "not an inhabitant of this world".

ALIEN GRAVEYARD

The alien is said to have been buried in the Aurora town cemetery, but the marking stone was deliberately removed to discourage people from disinterring the remains.

👁 *TEST YOUR KNOWLEDGE*

What did the military first say they had recovered and taken to the Roswell base?

A. Flying saucer

B. Flying disc

C. Flying balloon

D. Flying airship

What is the name of the extraterrestrial race from which the British royal family is descended, according to conspiracists?

A. Windsorians

B. Etonians

C. Draconians

D. Markovians

What lies at the centre of the Earth, according to hollow Earth believers?

A. Molten core

B. Smaller, second sun

C. Twin moons

D. UFO garage

What was the name of the US Air Force UFO investigation programme that ran from 1947 to 1969?

A. Project Black Book

B. Project Blue Book

C. Project Beige Book

D. Project Blank Book

What nationality is the philosopher who came up with the simulation hypothesis?

A. British

B. French

C. Norwegian

D. Swedish

How were Barney and Betty Hill's memories of their alien abduction retrieved?

A. Mind-control drugs

B. MK-Ultra

C. Hypnosis

D. Regression therapy

In which English county did the late Christmas visitors appear?

A. Norfolk

B. Suffolk

C. Essex

D. Surrey

What colour was the world of the Woolpit children?

A. Blue

B. Purple

C. Yellow

D. Green

How many UFOs are said to have followed Japan Airlines flight 1628 for 400 miles?

A. 1

B. 3

C. 7

D. Over 30

Which space probes first took the images of faces on Mars?

A. Viking

B. Gemini

C. Cassini

D. Apollo

Which workmen spotted aliens near a Finnish lake?

A. Electricians

B. Lumberjacks

C. Fishermen

D. Carpenters

What did the alien spacecraft crash destroy in Aurora, Texas, as well as a windmill?

A. Bakery

B. Well

C. Flower garden

D. Vegetable patch

CHAPTER EIGHT
CRYPTIDS AND PARANORMAL PHENOMENA

Does a colossal serpent lurk beneath the murky depths of Loch Ness? Or a hairy giant roam the dense forests of North America? This chapter dives into the realm of cryptozoology and the captivating world of cryptids — creatures that may or may not exist.

We explore a range of marvellously mysterious beasts, from the iconic Loch Ness Monster and elusive Bigfoot to lesser-known oddities like the Fresno Nightcrawlers and the bizarre Hopkinsville Goblins. We also delve into reports of phantom big cats stalking the countryside, the terrifying Mongolian Death Worm and the winged terror known as Mothman.

LOCH NESS MONSTER

The Loch Ness Monster, aka Nessie, has captivated imaginations for centuries. Tales of a beast lurking in the murky depths of Loch Ness in Scotland have been circulating since the seventh century.

Interest deepened in 1934 with a grainy photograph that claimed to show a long neck emerging from the water, and although the photo was exposed as a hoax, alleged sightings of a serpentine creature with humps and a tail continued to thrive and gain global attention.

Some loch-watchers believe that Nessie is a plesiosaur, a marine reptile long thought extinct, while others say it may be a giant eel, catfish or sturgeon. Certainly, the loch's depth of 230 metres is the perfect environment for a creature to remain hidden.

SCIENTIFIC RESEARCH

In 2019, researchers conducted environmental DNA analysis of the loch's water. While no evidence of a giant creature emerged, it did reveal an abundance of Atlantic salmon, a species not previously known to thrive in such large numbers within the loch.

BIGFOOT

Bigfoot, also known as Sasquatch, is the ultimate hairy wilderness dweller. This hulking two-legged creature is said to roam the remote forests of North America, particularly the Pacific Northwest. There are many theories surrounding the existence of Bigfoot.

- In Native American folklore, many tribes have legends of giant, hairy humanoids that inhabit the wilderness.

- Some people say that Bigfoot is a new species of primate unknown to science and that governments fear the societal and ecological impact of revealing its existence.

- Others believe that Bigfoot possesses unique intelligence or even psychic abilities, making it a threat or resource that the government wants to control.

CAUGHT ON CAMERA

The famous Patterson—Gimlin film from 1967 showed footage of a large, ape-like figure walking through a clearing. Though widely debated, the authenticity of the footage has never been definitively disproved.

THE FRESNO NIGHTCRAWLERS

The mystery that surrounds sightings of the Fresno Nightcrawlers has been a popular source of discussion on the internet in recent years. Some people describe the Nightcrawlers as terrifying-sounding, hairless, two-legged creatures, roughly the size of a large dog, with glowing red eyes, while others say they look like a pair of long-legged trousers.

Shaky overnight footage taken by a resident in the Californian city of Fresno in 2006 sparked a wave of curiosity and led people to theorize about a mutated breed of coyote, a government experiment gone wrong or even an extraterrestrial visitor. Despite the fervour, no concrete evidence of the Nightcrawlers has ever been found.

IS IT A COYOTE?

Fresno is home to coyotes, some of which suffer from mange, a skin disease that causes hair loss. Some commentators speculate that a mangy coyote on its hind legs, searching for food, could, in dim light, appear hairless and bipedal.

THE HOPKINSVILLE GOBLINS

The Hopkinsville incident of 1955 is a remarkable tale of a terrifying extraterrestrial encounter. On a quiet night near Hopkinsville in rural Kentucky, a local family called the Suttons say they were besieged by small, gremlin-like creatures with glowing red eyes who had emerged from a spacecraft.

The beings, described as about three feet tall with wrinkled, dark skin and claw-like hands, terrorized the family for several hours, popping up at their doorways and windows. The Suttons said they fired shots at the creatures and claimed to have wounded one of them, but no physical evidence of the goblins was ever found.

Some UFO researchers speculate that what the Suttons really saw were great horned owls, which stand up to two feet tall, are nocturnal, have yellow eyes and aggressively defend their nests.

THE DOVER DEMON

In 1977, in Dover, Massachusetts, a 17-year-old boy called Bill Bartlett claimed to have encountered a hairless, orange-skinned creature with glowing red eyes and tendril-like fingers while driving at night. Another boy in the area reported a similar encounter on the same night, and a teenage girl spotted the creature the following evening.

All the children sketched pictures of what they had seen. Bartlett's picture, in particular, bore an uncanny resemblance to archetypal big-headed aliens. Although the police suspected a schoolyard prank, the Dover Demon moniker stuck, and it has made its way into both horror movies and comics.

ANOTHER OWL?

Some people believe that, as in the Hopkinsville Goblins incident, the most likely explanation is that the children saw a snowy owl, its eyes reflecting a reddish peach colour from the car headlights.

PHANTOM CATS

Phantom cats are large, unidentified felines that prowl in areas and countries far beyond their natural habitats. Sightings of such beasts have been reported across the globe, from the remote British moors to the dense Australian outback but also including environments as diverse as China, Denmark, India and Switzerland.

Some people claim that these mysterious predators are pumas or panthers, or perhaps undiscovered species surviving in secret. Famous examples of phantom cats include:

- Beast of Bodmin – the most famous big cat in Britain, this panther-like creature is said to roam the moors at night.

- Blue Mountains Panther – this beast is claimed to be descended from circus or zoo escapees in Australia.

- Dayton Area Phantom Panther – black, leopard-like cats have been reported in Ohio, US.

- Gippsland Phantom Cat – it is claimed that an American World War Two airman released pumas into the Australian bush, after using them as mascots during the war.

MONGOLIAN DEATH WORM

Imagine a monstrous red worm that reaches up to five feet long. It lurks beneath the sand and spits acidic venom, leaps huge distances and has the power to electrocute its prey. These are just some of the theories that surround the Mongolian Death Worm of the Gobi Desert.

Scientists who study unconfirmed species of animals – cryptozoologists – have set up expeditions into the desert to find proof of the worm's existence.

However, some sceptics put the theories down to desert lore that has been embellished over time or suggest a simple case of mistaken identity, namely a confusion with real desert dwellers like the legless lizard, which can grow up to two feet long.

DESERT LORE

The Gobi Desert is nicknamed the "Graveyard of Dinosaurs" and has yielded some of the most significant dinosaur discoveries ever made, including the fearsome Velociraptor and the colossal Titanosaurus.

JERSEY DEVIL

Just the thought of the Jersey Devil, a nightmarish creature lurking in the desolate Pine Barrens of New Jersey in the US, has been terrifying people for over 250 years.

Legend pins the blame for its origin on Mother Leeds, a local woman burdened by an unwanted thirteenth pregnancy. In a fit of despair, she is said to have cursed the child as "the Devil's spawn". When the child was born, it transformed into the Jersey Devil and flew off into the night.

Claimed sightings of the beast over the years have fuelled theories of its actual existence, with physical descriptions varying from a kangaroo-like beast with bat wings to a demonic dog with a forked tail, or a reptilian monstrosity.

ICE COLD

The Jersey Devil has lent its name to two professional ice hockey teams. One stopped playing in 1973, but the New Jersey Devils of the National Hockey League are still going strong.

MOTHMAN

The Mothman of Point Pleasant, West Virginia, entered the world's consciousness in November 1966 when sightings of a large, human-like creature with glowing red eyes and enormous wings set nerves jangling.

Witnesses described the creature as lurking in the shadows, only to spring out and follow cars at high speeds. The local frenzy reached a fever pitch in December 1967 when the Silver Bridge, a major road connecting Point Pleasant to Ohio, collapsed and killed 46 people. Fear gripped the town, with many believing the Mothman was the culprit.

FILM FAME

John Keel wrote a book about the creature and its role in the bridge collapse in 1975. The Mothman Prophecies was later made into a film starring Richard Gere and Laura Linney.

MOTHS TO A FLAME

Since 2002, the people of Point Pleasant have embraced the Mothman, holding an annual festival, complete with costume contests, a Mothman prophecy contest and Mothman pizza.

CHUPACABRA

The Chupacabra is said to be a vicious predator with a thirst for livestock blood. It is said to roam the Americas, in particular the US, Mexico and Puerto Rico. The name Chupacabra is the Spanish for "goat-sucker".

There are many alleged victims of this ghoulish creature but a significant lack of hard evidence. There are no definitive photos or traces, but this has not diminished the creature's stature as a cult figure in the Americas.

CHUPACABRA CHEAT SHEET

- Some accounts depict a reptilian beast with spines and glowing eyes, while others suggest a hairless, dog-like form, around one metre tall.
- Many reports include a trail of drained carcasses, primarily goats, left behind in the creature's wake.
- Some believe the goat-sucker to be an extraterrestrial visitor, which crash-landed and now preys on local animals.

ORANG MAWAS

Deep within the Malaysian rainforest, sightings of a shadowy primate species known as the Orang Mawas have been recorded since 1871. The Orang Mawas are bipedal ape-like creatures of towering height, up to ten feet tall, and are said to be reclusive and extremely intelligent. In their native language, the local Orang Asli people call them the "Snaggle-Toothed Ghosts".

There is no doubt that descriptions of them bear a close resemblance to the orangutan, although local witnesses would be experienced enough to tell the difference between the two species.

Some people claim that the Orang Mawas possess a hidden civilization within the rainforest, pointing to discoveries of seemingly man-made stone structures deep within the jungle.

ANCIENT GIANTS

One theory suggests that the Orang Mawas are a remnant population of Gigantopithecus, an extinct primate species known for its immense size. However, fossil records appear to show that Gigantopithecus were knuckle-walkers, in contrast to the bipedal Orang Mawas.

⊙ TEST YOUR KNOWLEDGE

What type of extinct animal do some loch-watchers believe Nessie to be?

A. Velociraptor

B. Brontosaurus

C. Plesiosaur

D. Tyrannosaurus rex

When was the most convincing evidence of Bigfoot filmed?

A. 1935

B. 1946

C. 1967

D. 1982

What is the true identity of the Fresno Nightcrawler, according to some commentators?

A. Dog with mange

B. Coyote with mange

C. Owl with mange

D. Deer with mange

What colour were the Hopkinsville Goblins' eyes?

A. Blue

B. Red

C. Green

D. Yellow

When did Bill Bartlett spot the Dover Demon?

A. 1870

B. 1915

C. 1950

D. 1977

Who is said to have released the Gippsland Phantom Cat into the Australian outback?

A. Scottish sailor

B. American airman

C. Japanese farmer

D. Indian soldier

The Mongolian Death Worm is said to have what incredible power?

A. Electrocution

B. Invisibility

C. Flight

D. Superspeed

The Jersey Devil is said to be the thirteenth child of which woman?

A. Mother Fields

B. Mother Bradford

C. Mother Sheffield

D. Mother Leeds

For which tragic event in Point Pleasant history might the Mothman be responsible?

A. Baseball stadium fire

B. Bridge collapse

C. Earthquake

D. Wildfire

What does Chupacabra mean in Spanish?

A. Sheep-sucker

B. Cow-biter

C. Pig-sucker

D. Goat-sucker

How tall are the mysterious Orang Mawas of the Malaysian rainforest?

A. 3 ft

B. 6 ft

C. 10 ft

D. 20 ft

What sport do the Jersey Devils play in the US?

A. Baseball

B. American football

C. Soccer

D. Ice hockey

CONCLUSION

Hopefully you have enjoyed *The Conspiracy Theory Trivia Book* and learned more about some of the world's most bizarre mysteries. From the alleged fakery of the Moon landing to enigmatic lights in the skies, this book has been your guide through the labyrinthine world of conspiracy theories.

We've explored the shadowy corners of Area 51, questioned the influence of secret societies like the Illuminati and pondered the possibility of extraterrestrial involvement in everything from the pyramids to Roswell.

This book has barely scratched the surface of humanity's fascination with conspiracy theories. While a healthy dose of scepticism is vital, it is important to remain open to new ideas. Even seemingly outlandish conspiracy theories stem from a desire for answers, so think critically and consider the evidence carefully for yourself.

Wishing you happy trails – and a distinct absence of Chupacabras on your journey!

ANSWERS

CHAPTER ONE

Why do conspiracists believe the flag in the Moon-landing footage is proof that it was faked?
b) It is fluttering

In how many human generations do conspiracists believe a baby will be born without a skeleton, owing to fluoride poisoning?
b) 7

Which of these do conspiracists not suggest as the real reason behind chemtrails?
d) Nazi weapons testing

Which Nazi long-range missile may have been the precursor to Hitler's spaceship?
b) V-2

When was the Centennial Light first switched on?
c) 1901

Who was behind the MK-Ultra programme?
b) CIA

How many reactors experienced meltdowns in the Fukushima Daiichi nuclear power plant in Japan?
c) Three

What did market researcher James Vicary attempt to influence moviegoers to consume more of?
b) Popcorn

In 1776, an inoculation of which disease protected a boy against smallpox?
c) Cowpox

What theory lies at the heart of the claim that Peak Oil is a conspiracy by oil companies and governments?
c) Oil is a renewable resource

What was the name of the nightclub operator who killed Lee Harvey Oswald?
b) Jack Ruby

Which dangerous event do conspiracists believe the Large Hadron Collider may bring about?
c) Creation of a black hole

CHAPTER TWO

Which of these is not a defence measure at Area 51?
d) Automatic machine-gun turrets

What is a tell-tale sign of the Men in Black?
a) No fingernails

Which book does the phrase "Big Brother" come from?
c) *Nineteen Eighty-Four*

What was Barack Obama's career before moving into politics?
c) Civil rights attorney

When did sightings of the infamous black helicopters begin?
b) 1970s

How high were the waves in the Boxing Day Tsunami?
c) 30 m

Which Alaskan project do conspiracists believe may be a mind-control device?
a) HAARP

If Bill Clinton really is a robot, who is operating him, according to conspiracy theorists?
c) FBI

Why might the British government make it rain?
a) To control civilian behaviour

What do conspiracists believe are causing Californian wild fires?
d) Space lasers

Where do scientists believe Ebola originated from?
c) Fruit bats

Which British prime minister is alleged to have spied on their own cabinet using the Echelon programme?
c) Margaret Thatcher

CHAPTER THREE

When was the original Illuminati society formed?
a) 1776

Who does the New World Order want to do away with?
b) Middle classes

Which airport to conspiracists believe may be the headquarters of the Illuminati?
b) Denver

How many Yale students join the Skull and Bones society each spring?
c) 15

In which country did the *Protocols of the Elders of Zion* first appear?
d) Russia

Why do conspiracy theorists believe that cash may be on the way out?
c) To control humanity

Which book in the Bible appears to denounce implanted microchips as the Devil's work?
b) The Book of Revelation

In which century did the Freemasons originate?
b) The seventeenth century

How many lanes does the purported superhighway have that will link the countries of the North American Union?
c) 12

For what purpose do conspiracists believe that global recessions are deliberately caused?
d) To usher in the New World Order

What is the name of the society tasked with safeguarding the truth about Jesus's bloodline?
b) Priory of Sion

According to some conspiracy theorists, what is really causing global warming?
c) Changes in solar activity

<u>CHAPTER FOUR</u>

Who do conspiracy theorists believe may have built the pyramids?
c) Extraterrestrials

Which base system does the Maya Long Count calendar use?
d) Base-20

How old are the Nazca Lines?
a) At least 1,500 years old

Which philosopher first wrote about Atlantis?
b) Plato

What do conspiracists claim that the Chelyabinsk meteor really was?
a) Millennia-old alien spacecraft

How many years of history were just made up, according to the Phantom Time Hypothesis?
d) 300

Radiocarbon dating has revealed that the Turin Shroud originates in which time period?
c) The Middle Ages

How old was Elizabeth I when she died, according to conspiracy theorists?
a) 3

In which year did Bérenger Saunière take charge of the church in Rennes-le-Château?
b) 1885

Which woman do conspiracists believe may have been the real William Shakespeare?
b) Queen Elizabeth I

What is the name of the Anunnaki home planet?
d) Nibiru

According to conspiracists, what does the Turin Shroud reveal about Jesus that made the Church want to discredit it by falsifying the radiocarbon date?
b) He survived the Crucifixion

<u>CHAPTER FIVE</u>

Who did *The Simpsons* predict would be the US president some day?
a) Donald Trump

In which year did the real Avril Lavigne die, according to the Lavigne clone theory?
b) 2003

Why did Elvis fake his own death, according to some conspiracy theorists?
c) To avoid being killed by the Mafia

Approximately how many passengers and crew survived the *Titanic* disaster?
c) 700

In which year did Kurt Cobain die?
a) 1994

Conspiracy theorists believe that a photograph taken in 1898 shows that Greta Thunberg is a time traveller sent to warn us of the dangers of climate change. Where was the photograph taken?
b) Yukon

Which politician do some conspiracists believe may have been involved in Marilyn Monroe's death?
c) Castro

Who else was John Lennon's assassin planning to kill?
b) David Bowie

In which year was New Coke launched, to resounding boos?
b) 1985

How old was Bruce Lee when he died?
c) 32

Nobel Prize-winning author Albert Camus died in a car accident, but who do some conspiracists believe may have been behind his death?
a) KGB

What age are pop musicians most likely to die at, according to conspiracists?
c) 27

<u>CHAPTER SIX</u>

In which year did QAnon first explode on to the internet?
c) 2017

What was the nationality of the newspaper in which the first interview connecting 5G and Covid-19 appeared?
d) Belgian

What do conspiracy theorists fear that cryptocurrencies may bring about?
b) Loss of all personal privacy

What do flat Earth maps place at the perimeter of the Earth?
b) Antarctica

What did Alexa mistakenly order in 2017, while listening in to a conversation?
b) Doll's house

Which British vote first saw the #Pencilgate hashtag used?
c) Scottish independence referendum

Why was the Trans-Siberian railway built, according to conspiracy theorists?
c) To transport fish to Japan

Some conspiracists believe that the passengers of flight AF447 were kidnapped and taken to work in coal mines in which US state?
b) Colorado

What kind of restaurant did conspiracy theorists once believe housed a child sex ring?
b) Pizza

How quickly do some people believe AI will achieve superintelligence, once it is as clever as an average human?
a) Within minutes

Where does the theory that Finland does not exist originate?
d) Reddit

What did conspiracists take as a sign that thousands of paedophiles would soon be arrested?
b) Donald Trump sipping water

CHAPTER SEVEN

What did the military first say they had recovered and taken to the Roswell base?
b) Flying disc

What is the name of the extraterrestrial race from which the British royal family is descended, according to conspiracists?
c) Draconians

What lies at the centre of the Earth, according to hollow Earth believers?
b) Smaller, second sun

What was the name of the US Air Force UFO investigation programme that ran from 1947 to 1969?
b) Project Blue Book

What nationality is the philosopher who came up with the simulation hypothesis?
d) Swedish

How were Barney and Betty Hill's memories of their alien abduction retrieved?
c) Hypnosis

In which English county did the late Christmas visitors appear?
b) Suffolk

What colour was the world of the Woolpit children?
d) Green

How many UFOs are said to have followed Japan Airlines flight 1628 for 400 miles?
b) 3

Which space probes first took the images of faces on Mars?
a) Viking

Which workmen spotted aliens near a Finnish lake?
b) Lumberjacks

What did the alien spacecraft crash destroy in Aurora, Texas, as well as a windmill?
c) Flower garden

CHAPTER EIGHT

What type of extinct animal do some loch-watchers believe Nessie to be?
c) Plesiosaur

When was the most convincing evidence of Bigfoot filmed?
c) 1967

What is the true identity of the Fresno Nightcrawler, according to some commentators?
b) Coyote with mange

What colour were the Hopkinsville Goblins' eyes?
b) Red

When did Bill Bartlett spot the Dover Demon?
d) 1977

Who is said to have released the Gippsland Phantom Cat into the Australian outback?
b) American airman

The Mongolian Death Worm is said to have what incredible power?
a) Electrocution

The Jersey Devil is said to be the thirteenth child of which woman?
d) Mother Leeds

For which tragic event in Point Pleasant history might the Mothman be responsible?
b) Bridge collapse

What does Chupacabra mean in Spanish?
d) Goat-sucker

How tall are the mysterious Orang Mawas of the Malaysian rainforest?
c) 10 ft

What sport do the Jersey Devils play in the US?
d) Ice hockey

If you're interested in finding
out more about our books, find us
on Facebook at **Summersdale Publishers**,
on Twitter/X at **@Summersdale** and on Instagram and
TikTok at **@Summersdalebooks** and get in touch.
We'd love to hear from you.

www.summersdale.com